THE
MILLENNIAL
GENERATION

T H E

MILLENNIAL

GENERATION

LEADING TODAY'S YOUTH INTO THE FUTURE

VAUGHN J. FEATHERSTONE

DESERET BOOK COMPANY • SALT LAKE CITY, UTAH

Library of Congress Cataloging-in-Publication Data

Featherstone, Vaughn J.
    The millennial generation : leading today's youth into the future
/ Vaughn J. Featherstone.
        p.   cm.
    Includes bibliographical references and index.
    ISBN 1-57345-524-5
    1. Church work with youth—Mormon Church. 2. Mormon youth—
Religious life. I. Title.
BX8643.Y6F45   1999
259'.23—dc21   99-10519
                                                                CIP

Printed in the United States of America   72082-6463

10 9   8   7   6   5   4   3   2   1

This book is dedicated to the most important generation of youth leaders in any dispensation. To all of you who serve in stake presidencies, high councils, bishoprics, and stake and ward presidencies of young men and young women; to all advisers and Scout leaders; and especially to you parents, I express my gratitude for the work you have done but, far more important, for the work you will do for the youth of the next millennium. I include my 33 grandchildren, and others to be born, who are under your care. May this volume provide you with a vision of this noble task.

God bless you all as we enter the coming millennium.

Contents

Preface   ix

Acknowledgments   xi

Part 1: LEADING IN DOCTRINE   1

  1. Youth of the Coming Millennium   3

  2. To Understand the Aaronic Priesthood of God   10

  3. Justice Is Merciful, and Mercy Is Just   16

  4. God's Divine Mercy   23

  5. Joy Unspeakable   27

Part 2: LEADING IN PRINCIPLE   35

  6. The Deepest Convictions of Your Life   37

  7. Let the Temple Touch Our Youth   42

  8. Communicating in the Next Millennium   48

  9. "Men without Chests"   55

10. God Pains with Their Tears   60

11. Healing the Scars of Abuse   68

Part 3: LEADING IN PRACTICE   77

12. "The Strength of God Is in Us"   79

13. "For We Wrestle Not Against Flesh and Blood"   86

14. The Sins of Babylon 94

15. Seminary—a Godsend 100

16. "And the Day Shall Come That the Earth Shall Rest" 107

17. It's a Privilege to Serve a Mission 113

Part 4: LEADING IN CHARACTER 121

18. Some Things Never Change 123

19. Teach Youth to Be Kind 129

20. "Good Kid" Tools 137

21. The Victory of Good over the Tyranny of Evil 143

22. Elect Ladies 152

Index 159

Preface

I would be hard-pressed to estimate how many times I have spoken to youth groups or how many youth I have spoken to in all the varied settings during the approximately 25 years I have been called to work closely with the youth of the Church. I chaired Philmont Scout training for 16 years and attended national and world jamborees, youth conferences, firesides, morningsides, and Aaronic Priesthood and Young Women encampments. I have loved the assignment to work with the youth.

As I contemplated one last contribution I could make to the youth of the Church worldwide, I decided it was time to write this book. I am not writing it *to* the youth, I am writing it *for* the youth but *to* the adult leaders of youth. That is what I did with *A Generation of Excellence,* a book that I wrote more than 25 years ago.

This is my "King Benjamin's discourse" to those who will lead the youth into the next millennium. I believe my years of service have given me insight and understanding that I would like to share with every mother and father, every stake and mission president, every bishop and branch president, every Aaronic Priesthood and Young Women adviser, every high councilor and stake Young Men presidency member, and, hopefully, every coach, teacher, and lover of youth.

It is also written to the greatest generation of parents God has ever had on the earth. I hope it will bring peace and comfort as well as serve as a guide and counsel.

I think I will not write another book. I would like this to be the culmination of my service to the youth of the Church, and especially to the youth of the next millennium. I love them so! I have tried my best to serve the young people of this church well, to make myself available, and to be what President Harold B. Lee described as "a champion of youth." I know that I taught, loved, and prayed for the youth with all the energy of my soul.

God bless you wonderful men and women who will love, teach, train, and guide the greatest generation of youth yet to dwell on this earth. I offer this book to you with my profound love for them.

Acknowledgments

My personal thanks to Sylvia Tucker, who typed the manuscript of this book for me, assisted in the editing, and otherwise provided monumental help.

Also to Jack Lyon for his keen editorial eye and guidance in preparing the manuscript for publishing.

A special thanks to our thirty-three grandchildren—twenty-five boys and eight girls—who have given me sufficient motivation to write this book for their generation.

PART

1

....

LEADING IN DOCTRINE

Youth of the Coming Millennium

In the 29th chapter of Genesis is a beautiful thought that could be applied to any number of relationships: "And Jacob served seven years for Rachel; and they seemed but a few days, for the love he had to her" (verse 20). A volume of tender and deep feelings are expressed in that one sweet sentiment.

About 30 years ago Elder Marion D. Hanks gave a marvelous talk about the youth of the Church. It carried such power in my life and in the lives of many leaders over the years that I have heard it referred to over and over again. Elder Hanks recounted the story of Jacob's sons going to Egypt to obtain food. Pharaoh had promised Joseph: "Forasmuch as God hath shewed thee all this [the seven fat and the seven lean years], there is none so discreet and wise as thou art: Thou shalt be over my house, and according unto thy word shall all my people be ruled: only in the throne will I be greater than thou" (Genesis 41:39–40).

You will recall that years later, Joseph's brothers came to Egypt to buy food. Joseph, whom they did not recognize, told his brothers to bring down the youngest brother, Benjamin, or they would not be given food. When they approached their father, Israel, with this request, he said, "Ye know that my wife [Rachel] bare me two sons: and the one went out from me, and I said, Surely he is torn in pieces; and I saw him not since: and if ye take this [Benjamin] also from me, and mischief befall him, ye shall bring down my gray hairs with sorrow to the grave" (Genesis 44:27–29).

All of this was explained to Joseph, who had worked out a plan to hold Benjamin behind while the others returned to Jacob. These marvelous words, which Elder Hanks shared with such tenderness and deep feelings, came from Judah, an older brother, to Joseph: "Now therefore, I pray thee, let thy servant abide instead of the lad a bondman to my lord; and let the lad go up with his brethren. *For how shall I go up to my father, and the lad be not with me?*" (Genesis 44:33–34; emphasis added). Through all my years of service to the youth and my own family, those words have been with me.

During the time that I served as general president of the Young Men organization, President Ezra Taft Benson gave a marvelous talk directed to those who lead youth. He quoted from Isaiah 21:11:

"Watchman, what of the night? Watchman, what of the night?"

I recall the spiritual impact of these questions as if God had directed them to me personally.

Our daughter Jill and her husband, Brian, have four wonderful sons and a precious daughter. Jill is a sensitive, soft, dignified woman. She is perceptive. She wrote a letter to each of her six brothers and to us as parents. In essence she said, "This has been a real year of testing for all of us. It seems that trials have swept through each of our families." Further into her letter she said, "We need the Lord's blessings." Then she proposed that we show our faith in God by having a continuous chain of our family members being in the temple during one particular month. She suggested assigned dates for parents and also for our grandchildren who were old enough to do baptisms for the dead. During that month there were one or more members of our family in the temple every day it was open. There was a peace, a unity, a spiritual power that came to our whole family collectively. I do not know when we have ever felt as close as we did when we were appealing to God in a united effort and demonstrating our faith in the temple.

Someone said, "Use all of the tools in your tool box." We need to use all of our spiritual resources, including the temple, to serve this upcoming generation. You can feel the tenderness and desperation, and the deep feeling in a parent's heart, in these poetic words:

> Oh, Where is my wandering boy tonight?
> the boy of my tend'rest care:
> The boy that was once my joy and light,
> the child of my love and prayer.
>
> Once he was pure as the morning dew
> as he knelt at his mother's knee;
> No face was so bright, no heart more true,
> and none was as sweet as he.
>
> Oh, could I see him now, my boy
> as fair as in olden time;
> When prattle and smile made home a joy,
> and life was a merry chime.
>
> Go for my wandering boy tonight—
> go search for him where you will;
> But bring him to me with all his blight
> and tell him I love him still.
>
> Oh, where is my boy tonight? Where is my boy tonight?
> My heart o'erflows
> for I love him, he knows,
> Oh, where is my boy tonight?
> (Author unknown.)

I find it difficult to get through that poem, for I feel the parental love so deeply. We need to teach so much to our youth because of the many pitfalls facing this generation. One of the greatest concerns we have for our youth is the perversion of all that is holy and pure. Consider the contrast between what our youth hear from the world and President Boyd K. Packer's teaching that "romance is deeply and significantly religious." That is a wonderful thought. He also stated that "romance is essential to exaltation." We need to teach the purity of this beautiful concept.

Ella Wheeler Willcox wrote:

> It is easy enough to be virtuous
> When nothing tempts you to stray,

When without or within, no voice of sin
Is luring your soul away;
But it is only a negative virtue
Until it is tried by fire,
For the soul that is worth the honor of earth
Is the one that resists desire.

There is a luring that is satanically inspired by all the lusts of the world. We need to teach our youth what Pericles said: "Surely the bravest are those who have the clearest vision of what is before them, both danger and glory alike and yet, notwithstanding, move forward to meet it."

When we have faith we need not fear. As we raise up this special generation we need to teach them the power that comes through virtue.

Our youth are clean, handsome, beautiful, beyond compare in all the world. We need to be there for them when they need a guide, a warning. Shakespeare puts the following words into the mouth of Tarquin (Sextus Tarquinius, the king's son) in his epic poem "The Rape of Lucrece." They are sobering and reflect his knowledge of Christ's teachings. If only our youth were taught and understood the emptiness that comes when they seek happiness through sin.

What win I if I gain the thing I seek—
a dream, a breath, a froth of fleeting joy?
Who buys a minute's mirth to wail a week,
or sells eternity to get a toy?
For one sweet grape, who will the vine destroy?
Or what fond beggar, but to touch the crown
Would with the scepter straight be strucken down?

Then the words of Lucrece:

Thy secret pleasure turns to open shame
Thy private feasting to a public fast,
Thy smoothing titles to a ragged name.

Teach our beloved youth there is great truth in these words.

The book of Proverbs states: "Then shalt thou walk in thy way safely, and thy foot shall not stumble" (Proverbs 3:23).

You will find in life that peace and direction come from being involved in a cause. During the time that my wife and I served in the

Philippines, we went to the Memorial Day Service held at the American Cemetery in Manila. I believe it was General Ramos, prior to his election as president, who told of a true heroic deed during the Second World War. The Japanese had occupied the Philippines. Several Filipino soldiers had been captured and were going before a firing squad. One of them asked the commanding officer if he could play one number on his accordion before he was executed. Permission was granted. This young Filipino soldier walked over, picked up his accordion, walked back, stood in line with the other condemned men, and then played loudly, clearly, and beautifully, singing these words:

> God Bless America, land that I love
> Stand beside her and guide her
> Through the night
> With a light from above.
> From the mountains to the prairies
> To the oceans white with foam.
> God Bless America, my home sweet home.

The shots rang out, and this young hero lay dead—a true patriot. Teach youth about values, patriotism, spirituality, courtesy, and kindness by observing real-life models and examples.

As a young man I was invited by Larraine Arnell to go to the hospital to administer to a sweet, little old lady. I memorized the words for the anointing prayer. It was beautiful and simple. We went to the hospital. The little widow was humbled that we had come. Larraine Arnell said, "Why don't we kneel by the bed and say a prayer." He invited me to offer the prayer. After the prayer I anointed her head with consecrated oil, and Larraine Arnell sealed the anointing with a beautiful blessing. At the end of the blessing I looked up and saw tears on the cheeks of Brother Arnell. He bent down and kissed the cheek of this sweet little widow, and a tear dropped off his cheek onto hers.

Since that day I have hardly given a blessing in a hospital or to someone who was sick that I have not felt again that same sweet spirit, and I have bent down and kissed the forehead or cheek of the man, woman, or child, and quite often I have left a tear there also. What a wonderful blessing Larraine Arnell's example was.

Grady Bogue, a university professor, said: "Rightly done, teaching

7

is a precious work. It is, however, the one human endeavor most damaging in consequences when done without care or competence. To carry a student in harm's way because of either ignorance or arrogance—because we do not know or do not care—is an act far worse than a bungled surgery. Our mistake will not bleed. Instead it will carry hidden scars where mean and tragic consequences may not be seen until years have passed and remedy is painful and/or impossible" (*Vital Speeches,* 1988, p. 615).

Life is not easy. We will each be tested to the limit, either personally or through those near and dear to us. If you have made a mistake, let us give you hope. Walter Malone understood the principles of mercy and forgiveness. He wrote the following poem, which is included in its entirety with his name in the Tennessee State Hall of Fame. If writing the poem were all he ever did, he deserves to have his name emblazoned in the Eternal Hall of Fame.

Opportunity

They do me wrong who say I come no more
When once I knock and fail to find you in.
For every day I stand outside your door
And bid you wake, and rise to fight and win.

Wail not for precious chances passed away,
Weep not for golden ages on the wane!
Each night I burn the records of the day;
At sunrise every soul is born again.

Laugh like a boy at splendors that have sped,
To vanished joys be blind and deaf and dumb;
My judgements seal the dead past with its dead,
But never binds a moment yet to come.

Though deep in mire, wring not your hands and weep;
I lend my arm to all who say "I can!"
No shame-faced outcast ever sank so deep
But yet might rise and be again a man!

Dost thou behold thy lost youth all aghast?
Dost reel from righteous retribution's blow?
Then turn from blotted archives of the past,
And find the future's pages white as snow.

> Art thou a mourner? Rouse thee from thy spell.
> Art thou a sinner? Sins may be forgiven.
> Each morning gives thee wings to flee from hell,
> Each night a star to guide thy feet to heaven!

And yet another poet said:

> Humpty Dumpty sat on a wall
> Humpty Dumpty had a great fall;
> And all the King's horses, and all the King's men
> Couldn't put Humpty together again.

But the King could, and the King can, and the King will.

In Isaiah we read: "Come now, and let us reason together saith the Lord; though your sins be as scarlet, they shall be as white as snow: though they be red like crimson, they shall be as wool" (Isaiah 1:18).

Oh, my beloved young friends, you are our youth of the next millennium. Use great leaders and your parents as models. Remember the strength that comes from virtue. Be brave and patriotic in whatever country you live, and remember you haven't made any unerasable mistakes. The Atonement is a fact, and the results are sure when we repent. Make the Master's cause your cause and surely you will find contentment, peace, and rejoicing.

We, all of the Brethren, love you, and we pray for you, and we will do all in our power to train and teach and prepare you at the dawning of this great and next millennium in preparation for eternal life.

2

To Understand the Aaronic Priesthood of God

When the Aaronic Priesthood is conferred on young men, they have the authority to minister in temporal affairs. Using the words *minister* and *serve* interchangeably will better fit our purpose here.

The Church and ward Aaronic Priesthood presidencies (Presiding Bishopric and ward bishopric) have the authority and keys to administer the temporal affairs of the kingdom in their various jurisdictions. They receive the tithes and offerings. They are responsible for the storehouse of food, clothing, finances, fuel, all member resources, medicines, and health care. The very essence of charity in the Church is welfare. Can there be a more Christlike service than providing for the hungry, naked, destitute, orphan, or widow? When we perform temporal service, we function in the authority of the Aaronic Priesthood.

Young men who hold the offices of either deacon, teacher, or priest may receive additional opportunities depending on their office in the Aaronic Priesthood. Members of the Aaronic Priesthood prepare, administer, and pass the sacrament. This holy ordinance ties directly to the Atonement of the Lord Jesus Christ and is entrusted to the Aaronic Priesthood. Priests can baptize, confer the Aaronic Priesthood, and ordain other deacons and teachers and priests. Aaronic Priesthood holders collect fast offerings, assist the bishop in distributing food, clothing, fuel, and other goods to the poor, and care for the chapel and grounds. In addition, they serve as home teachers, exhort the members to righteousness, keep the Church free from iniquity, and perform baptisms for the dead. They serve as messengers for the bishop and as ushers in meetings. They belong to a quorum, preside when called upon by the bishop, hold keys when president of a quorum, activate those not attending, and secure each other to the quorum through this brotherhood.

They understand and teach, knowing that the Aaronic Priesthood has the keys to the gospel of repentance and of baptism by immersion for the remission of sins. Constantly they are preparing to go to the temple worthily to do baptisms for the dead and then eventually to receive their endowment and prepare to serve a mission.

In quorums they teach each other the principles of the gospel. They plan quorum activities with a priesthood purpose. They determine how they will attend to the needs of the widow and orphan. They speak in sacrament meeting when invited. They bear testimony during fast and testimony meeting. Their responsibilities are in the preparatory priesthood—preparatory to functioning in the Melchizedek Priesthood, to finding a companion to take to the temple, and to becoming a father in Israel.

All of the above and much, much more, performed in the Lord's way, transforms this church into a church of welfare, a church that cares for the widow and orphan, and a church that ministers in a charitable way to all the needy.

As we continue to fulfill our stewardships to the fullest, the Church will take its rightful place as the most powerful force on the earth. This is a temporal world, and when the priesthood over temporal affairs moves forward unitedly to perform the great Aaronic Priesthood work, it will startle the world and bring forth a generation of youth as fair as the sun and clear as the moon. The army of Aaronic Priesthood will "become very great," will be sanctified before the Lord, and its "banners [will] be terrible unto all nations" (D&C 105:31).

Sometimes we forget to appreciate God's wisdom and the strength of His priesthood organization. Consider with me the following chart

11

that demonstrates what would happen if we put the full Aaronic Priesthood program into effect. For purposes of comparison let's look at both the Aaronic Priesthood organization and the Young Women organization.

Aaronic Priesthood Program	Young Women's Program
* Graduate from Primary	* Graduate from Primary into Young Women program
* Have Aaronic Priesthood conferred	* Father or bishopric member could give a blessing
* Belong to a quorum	* Belong to a class
* President of quorum set apart, holds keys	* Set apart as president over the class
* Aaronic priesthood quorum presidency responsible for all members of the quorum: • presides over quorum • encourages brotherhood • activates less-active members • teaches the quorum as assigned	* Class presidency responsible for all members of the class: • presides over class • encourages sisterhood • activates less-active members • teaches the class as assigned
* Attend presidency meeting weekly	* Attend presidency meeting weekly
* Hold keys of the ministering of angels, the gospel of repentance, and baptism by immersion	
* Prepare, bless, and administer the sacrament	
* Home teach assigned families each month	
* Collect fast offerings	
* Usher at meetings	* May usher at meetings
* Serve as bishop's messenger	

* Priests may baptize

* Priests may ordain other deacons, teachers, and priests

* Serve on bishop's youth committee (a priest co-chairs)

* Assist bishop in work of Aaronic Priesthood (welfare, widows, needy)

* Oath and covenant of the priesthood

* Achievement: Duty to God

* Mutual: combined YM-YW activities

* Baptisms for the dead

* Seminary enrollment: 4 years

* Receive blessings
  • Confirmation
  • Ordination to office of a deacon
  • Each time set apart in a presidency
  • Ordination to office of a teacher
  • Ordination to office of a priest
  • Ordination to Melchizedek Priesthood
  • Setting apart as full-time missionary

* Temple preparation

---

* Serve on the bishop's youth committee (a Laurel co-chairs)

* Charitable service to members, assist bishop

* Young Women Values, Young Women Theme

* Achievement: Young Women Personal Progress; Young Women Medallion

* Mutual: combined YW-YM activities

* Baptisms for the dead

* Seminary enrollment: 4 years

* Receive blessings
  • Confirmation
  • Each time set apart in a presidency
(Unless a bishop is very thoughtful or a young woman happens to be called into several presidencies, there is a chance she would not receive another blessing during her lifetime unless she requests one. Wouldn't it be wonderful if every young woman could receive a blessing at appropriate times in her life, or as she may request one?)

* Temple preparation

* Mission preparation: expected to serve

* Prepare for role as husband and father

The Aaronic Priesthood organization is the greatest organization on the earth for worthy young men. It can include camping, athletics, cultural events, and similar activities as part of the quorum activity program, and always with a priesthood purpose. The Scouting program is a support to this organization.

Every bishop and Young Men leader should fully implement the Aaronic Priesthood program. Every Aaronic Priesthood holder has a right to home teach, collect fast offerings, and participate in the ordinances of sacrament.

This is what God has provided for the young men of the Aaronic Priesthood in His Church.

* Mission preparation: only if she desires to serve

* Prepare for role as wife and mother

The Young Women program is based on values, activities, and achievements that lead young women to the temple. When followed as outlined, it is the finest program for young women in the world. It involves leadership, sisterhood, culture, sports, camping, service, and activities with a purpose.

The personal progress achievement program is critical to the success of each young woman. Mutual provides opportunities to socialize with the young men. The Young Women values are inspired. All young women should memorize them.

These programs for Aaronic Priesthood and Young Women are wonderful. They serve the needs of youth well. The one point I really want to emphasize is this: *If all we had for the young men of the Church was the Aaronic Priesthood with all its wonderful responsibilities and duties as well as quorum activities, we would have a free-standing, complete program for young men. The same is true for the Young Women program. It is a superb program. In addition, bishops and advisers need to be aware of the need to give blessings to young women every time an opportunity presents itself, such as graduating from class to class or as requested.*

This is a wonderful church. We also have an activity program that is supplemental to the Aaronic Priesthood. The presiding Brethren of the

14

Church have determined that in the United States and Canada, and in other countries and communities determined by local priesthood leaders, Scouting serves as an activity of the Aaronic Priesthood. In addition, for selected countries, an activity program for Young Men outside the United States and Canada has been approved. The local priesthood leaders determine which activity program they will implement.

Whichever activity program is chosen becomes an extension of the quorum. This is also true with competitive sports within the stake. They become an extension of the quorum. This eliminates separate programs competing for the time of the young men.

Now consider what the supplemental programs add to the Aaronic Priesthood.

SUPPLEMENTAL DIMENSIONS OF SCOUTING AND ACTIVITY PROGRAMS

• A Scouting achievement program involving rank-by-rank advancement

• Outdoor skills training, including survival and "no trace" camping

• Camping facilities and an organized camping program

• Award system (appealing to young men) that includes a court of honor to highlight achievements of individual young men

• Scout Oath and Law (provide inspiration and character building)

• Council and national activities, including jamborees (local, national, and world)

• Training for leaders furnished by the Scout organization

There are many more dimensions of Scouting, such as challenge courses, rappelling, spelunking, obstacle courses, river running, backpacking, fishing, and so forth that make the program very appealing to young men. The Activity Program for Young Men outside the United States and Canada also has these same dimensions of challenge and excitement and provides a powerful tool in holding young men close to the Church.

Now, in summary, the whole purpose of this chapter is simply to remind leaders that we have the greatest programs in the world for youth. All we need to do is fully implement them. When we do that as an entire Church, then we will have prepared our "generation of excellence" for the next millennium.

3

Justice Is Merciful, and Mercy Is Just

I have had an interesting mental struggle as I have tried to fully understand justice and mercy. Although I seem to be getting closer, there is still much to learn. Every priesthood holder and every sister in this Church should seek to understand the dimensions of justice and mercy. Our understanding of these two God-given doctrinal principles is essential to our ministering in the kingdom.

Parents and leaders, please teach the youth the message contained in this chapter. It may be more important to some than we would ever suppose. They need to understand justice and mercy.

In other works I have used Alma's statement that "the works of justice could not be destroyed, according to the supreme goodness of God" (Alma 12:32). I have marveled and had my vision enlarged by this beautiful description of justice by Alma. Of necessity justice must be a two-edged sword. A component part of justice is mercy. Justice is as merciful to the innocent as mercy is to the transgressor. Mercy is an integral part of justice, and the two cannot be separated.

In describing those who are unwilling to repent and have chosen evil, Jacob taught: "According to the power of justice, for justice cannot be denied, ye must go away into that lake of fire and brimstone, whose flames are unquenchable, and whose smoke ascendeth up forever and ever, which lake of fire and brimstone is endless torment" (Jacob 6:10). King Benjamin adds these words: "Therefore if that man repenteth not, and remaineth and dieth an enemy to God, the demands of divine justice do awaken his immortal soul to a lively sense of his own guilt, which doth cause him to shrink from the presence of the Lord, and doth fill his breast with guilt, and pain, and anguish, which is like an unquenchable fire" (Mosiah 2:38). It would only be just that a rebellious person, a transgressor, have a full understanding of his or her guilt and know that punishment is justified. That is where the endless torment will take place.

However, in the grand and great goodness of God, he has prepared a way for those who have rebelled and transgressed and then have come to a brighter recollection of the error and folly of their way and have chosen to follow the Redeemer and to repent of things done in the past.

Again King Benjamin has said: "I say unto you, if ye have come to a knowledge of the goodness of God, and his matchless power, and his wisdom, and his patience, and his long-suffering towards the children of men; and also, the atonement which has been prepared from the foundation of the world, that thereby salvation might come to him that should put his trust in the Lord, and should be diligent in keeping his commandments, and continue in the faith even unto the end of his life" (Mosiah 4:6).

The Atonement has certain requirements that we must meet in order to qualify for its blessings. It requires "trust in the Lord," diligence in keeping the commandments, continuing in faith, baptism, and then enduring unto the end of life. It is only just that transgressors and sinners demonstrate a change of heart and performance to match their repentance before the Atonement can become effective in their lives.

One of the great, merciful dimensions of justice comes to the innocent—the incest victim, those mourning the untimely death of a loved one, those with debilitating diseases, the quadriplegic, the parents of a wayward son or daughter, and the ten thousand more ways the innocent suffer.

An incest victim suffers beyond belief, especially a young child—so innocent, so trusting and believing. The mental and physical damage can be monumental. Add to that the stress and anger that come to the innocent when seemingly nothing is done by family members or priesthood leaders. In the years ahead comes the full understanding that maturity brings, and the victim has a far clearer vision of what could have been done by a mother, a bishop, or a relative to protect a defenseless child. Generally the victim desires to see the perpetrator suffer as he or she has. The burden the innocent carries increases. It includes not only the original violation, which has such a profound negative impact, but also the additional burden of knowing that the perpetrator is free, quite often active in the Church, sometimes even on a mission. The feeling that people should have given protection but apparently did not often adds greatly to the spiritual and emotional distress.

The same concerns are raised over others who suffer innocently—parents with wayward children, individuals with debilitating diseases or even paralysis, loved ones who die. Then it is that we must exclaim, "Thank God for the bountiful mercies claimed through justice!"

Abinadi, in one of the greatest sermons of all time, declared, "And thus God breaketh the bands of death, having gained the victory over death; giving the Son power to make intercession for the children of men." We might say here that intercession includes the innocent, who suffer not from the use of their agency but from conditions forced on them or beyond their control. Abinadi continues, "[Christ,] having ascended into heaven, having the bowels of mercy; being filled with compassion towards the children of men; standing betwixt them and justice" (Mosiah 15:8–9).

The Savior, filled with compassion and mercy, will ever reach out with loving arms to the innocent. That would only be just. In the 7th chapter of Alma we learn that the Atonement covers the innocent. Christ suffered pains, afflictions, and temptations, but he also took upon himself "the pains and the sicknesses of his people" and "their infirmities." Why? "That his bowels may be filled with mercy, according to the flesh, that he may know according to the flesh how to succor his people according to their infirmities" (Alma 7:11–12).

Through justice we may have an absolute assurance that the wicked, in the case of an incest perpetrator, for example, will not go unpunished. Justice demands that its ends be met. There will not be the tiniest violation or act overlooked. The price will be paid in full—every iota of offense will be brought to light, and either suffering or repentance will satisfy the full demands of justice.

Therefore, the innocent should not, must not, carry the additional burden of hate, anger, or desire for revenge. The beautiful blessing in justice is that it can be left to God, who will not vary. Nothing will be left undone. Following this counsel will bring a great measure of peace to the innocent victims.

The remaining pain and suffering to the innocent—which may have damaged the offended one spiritually, physically, and mentally—may also be swept away as the "dream of a night's vision." The healing process of charity cannot possibly be measured. "Now abideth faith, hope, charity, these three; but the greatest of these is charity" (1 Cor. 13:13). "Charity never faileth" (1 Cor. 13:8). "Charity is the pure love of Christ, and it endureth forever; and whoso is found possessed of it at the last day, it shall be well with him" (Moro. 7:47).

Charity would have us forgive those who have violated us. This sounds like hard doctrine, this forgiving someone who has done such abusive, evil things. But the scriptures promise us that forgiving is a merciful, charitable act that rewards the offended with peace.

Forgiving the offender takes great faith in Christ, but his promises are sure. There will come to the forgiving person an immeasurable peace and joy that will remove all the dark stains and scars, the hurt and anger, the frustration, and the emotional and physical damage as though it had never happened. Surely the Savior of the world—the one who healed the leper, the blind, the lame, the sick, and the palsied—can heal emotional sicknesses as well. He can and He will. There is a little verse I have used before. I am not certain of the author, but it has a great message:

> I believe the test of a great man is humility.
> I do not mean by humility the doubt in one's own personal
> power; but really, truly great men have the curious feeling that
> greatness is not in them but through them and they see
> divine in every other human soul and are foolishly, endlessly,
> incredibly merciful.

To forgive another requires a loftiness of spirit, a confidence in self, and a charitable and merciful heart. We do not have to wait until others have repented or even until they have been punished to forgive them. We can take responsibility as an "actor" rather than as a "reactor."

Those who have a difficult time forgiving a former spouse, child, or parent will find that the burden increases through the years. Some say, "I will never forgive this or that person." What a useless waste of mental and physical energy! How detrimental to health is such an attitude. Even some who understand the doctrine of justice will not leave it to God; thus they find themselves in Satan's grasp. He will use hate, anger, and a desire for revenge to destroy those who will not leave justice to God. Satan can never bring peace to a living soul.

Some accuse bishops and stake presidents of not taking action. Please understand that people can lie to a bishop, a stake president, even a General Authority. Remember that the problem is not with the priesthood leader—it is with the liar, the transgressor. Sometimes priesthood leaders have the gift of discernment and clearly understand when someone is lying or telling the truth. At other times the Spirit leaves a priesthood leader to struggle on his own. He may hear a convincing story from the victim and be persuaded that what was said is true. Then during an interview with the accused, denials may take place, and tears may flow. The priesthood leader may feel that one of the conflicting parties might be lying, but he may have enough doubt not to move forward. The individuals involved might simply have different perceptions or perhaps suffer from false memory syndrome. Possibly the Lord is forcing the leader to struggle for some divine reason we do not understand. Many priesthood leaders have been in that position. They plead and pray fervently, but sometimes the answers seem slow to come.

A good principle to remember is to ask what each party stands to gain from lying or telling the truth. The incest victim has humiliation, embarrassment, and fear to face by telling the truth, and usually nothing to gain by lying. The alleged abuser has everything to gain by lying and a disciplinary council to face by telling the truth. Nonetheless, although this is a helpful principle to follow, it is not foolproof. For example, I have seen some cases where accusations were made as a means of revenge following a nasty divorce. Unfortunately, in such cases the priesthood leader may have a difficult task determining what is true.

Remember the Savior's statement in speaking of a devil that his disciples could not cast out of a child: "This kind goeth not out but by

20

prayer and fasting" (Matthew 17:21). So it is with the liar. A priesthood leader can only do his conscientious best. Members would be wise to find fault not with their bishops but rather with the liar.

King Mosiah, the son of King Benjamin, helped us to understand when he said, "Now it is better that a man should be judged of God than of man, for the judgments of God are always just, but the judgments of man are not always just" (Mosiah 29:12). A man may lie to a priesthood leader and sometimes get away with it, but he cannot lie to the Spirit and hope for the same results. Therefore, God's judgments will always be based on all the facts, without bias or prejudice, and with total understanding. As the author of the laws of mercy and justice, he will make a perfect judgment. Why, oh why, can't we be content to let the God of heaven carry our burdens for us? He will if we will only ask.

Abinadi gave warning to "those who rebel, who have perished in their sins, those who have known the commandments and would not keep them" (Mosiah 15:26). Here we see God exercising justice, for Abinadi says unto such: "Therefore ought ye not to tremble? For salvation cometh to none such; for the Lord hath redeemed none such; yea, neither can the Lord redeem such" (Mosiah 15:27). And then Abinadi tells us why: "For he cannot deny himself; for he cannot deny justice when it has its claim" (ibid.). God is as bound by justice as we are and will be.

Justice is an extension, an integral part, of mercy. The innocent can be absolutely assured that the Righteous Judge of the universe will see that the demands of justice are met. On the other hand, even the innocent would want mercy extended to all who had repented and qualified for the blessings of the Atonement. Alma taught, "Mercy claimeth all which is her own"; however, then he added this qualifier to define those who would be claimed by mercy: "None but the truly penitent are saved" (Alma 42:24). Would the incest victim still demand justice, more than the Atonement could provide, if the person who had offended or violated her qualified as the "truly penitent"? Such an attitude would not be just. That is why we leave justice and mercy to God, and we instill in the innermost recesses of our hearts and souls the sincere qualities of charity, mercy, and forgiveness. That is the Savior's direction to all of us. Thus, whenever mercy is extended—no matter what the conditions— the full demands of justice will have been met, and mercy will claim "her own" through the Atonement. This is the highest order of justice. Mercy and justice are extensions of each other. To be merciful is just and to be just is merciful.

In the ninth chapter of 2 Nephi, Jacob says: "But, behold, the righteous, the saints of the Holy One of Israel, they who have believed in the Holy One of Israel, they who have endured the crosses of the world, and despised the shame of it [I believe this includes the innocent who suffer], they shall inherit the kingdom of God, which was prepared for them from the foundation of the world, and their joy shall be full forever" (verse 18). Then Jacob exclaims, "O how great the holiness of our God! For he knoweth all things, and there is not anything save he knows it" (verse 20).

When we can have that kind of confidence in our great and good God, then we can leave to him justice and mercy, and we can go on to increase our charity, love, mercy, and forgiveness as we become more like Him and "prepare [our] souls for that glorious day when justice shall be administered unto the righteous" (2 Nephi 9:46).

4

God's Divine Mercy

We mentioned in another chapter that justice and mercy are eternal principles extended to man through God's great goodness. We often discuss them as if they were opposites, as if there were a dividing line between them. But mercy is not complete without justice, and justice would forever be lacking without mercy. They are as inseparable as faith and repentance.

Justice is a form of mercy, and mercy is a form of justice. The innocent often suffer far, far more than the guilty. Alma describes justice "according to the supreme goodness of God" (see Alma 12:32). Many of God's children suffer through no fault of their own—those who have wayward children, the innocent spouse whose companion commits adultery, the victims of debilitating diseases, children born into poverty, those whose parents care not and love not. Mercy would demand for them the same blessings claimed by the transgressor. Justice according to the supreme goodness of God would require relief and peace equivalent to that extended the sinner who repents.

When the demands of justice are met, the innocent understand why Alma refers to this law as the "supreme goodness of God." The innocent victim is required by God, if he or she would find peace, to forgive the perpetrator and leave justice to God. This requires a depth of faith more penetrating than the inflicted evil and resultant scars. God, who administers justice, will not leave the guilty party free from suffering. The innocent one can be assured that the perpetrator will not receive forgiveness and will suffer exquisitely until the ends of justice are met. There will be no way around that one.

On the other hand, mercy would require that at some point justice will have been satisfied. And mercy would also expect full justice to the offender lest the innocent have suffered in vain. Thus, mercy makes claim on justice after the law is fulfilled. Mercy also is extended to bridge the gulf, which no man could cross. Through His divine mercy, Christ has fulfilled the demands of justice both on behalf of the transgressor and the innocent victim. His bowels are filled with a mercy that extends to every soul who will come unto Him. This includes all men whatever their evil deed, save it be the taking of innocent life or the denial of the Holy Ghost. Few will find the strait and narrow way that leads to life eternal. However, the way is clearly marked—messengers, prophets, apostles, and angels stand to clearly guide the way. So few—so very, very few—will follow the Savior of all mankind. But those few will receive and hold tight the word of God and will partake of the delicious fruit of the tree of life.

"The way for man is narrow, but it lieth in a straight course before him, and the keeper of the gate is the Holy One of Israel; and he employeth no servant there; and there is none other way save it be by the gate; for he cannot be deceived, for the Lord God is his name" (2 Nephi 9:41).

We need to teach youth who have been victims of rape, incest, sexual abuse, and similar tragedy that there is no transgression or wrongdoing on their part. No one can forcibly take our virtue or character. They may violate us, but in the eyes of God there is no loss of virginity, no loss of chastity, no loss of character. The only way we can lose our virtue or character is by our own free will and volition.

This is an important principle for our youth to remember. Such victims need no repentance because there has been no transgression on their part. The perpetrator is the violator and must unavoidably suffer the demands of justice. But the innocent are without blemish no matter what act is forced on them.

I have come to love justice equally as much as mercy. As I have traversed the earth I have met multitudes of Saints who have suffered innocently when seemingly the perpetrator went his or her own way without a particle of remorse. Justice is "according to the supreme goodness of God." Justice is the very essence of mercy. Mercy could never be justified in claiming the unrepentant and the wicked without the proper administration of justice. And justice must be satisfied when the full demands of the law are met. Thus, justice is mercy and mercy is justice.

When the perpetrator receives the penalty required by justice, this also extends mercy to the innocent victim. The knowledge that some form of suffering or repentance is required of the perpetrator to fulfill the demands of justice is an exquisite extension of mercy to the one violated. He or she can have full confidence that justice will be demanded by a perfect Judge, who will know the depths of repentance suffered by the guilty party, as well as the guilt of those who come before Him unrepentant.

Thus, our youth may be assured that as they forgive those who have violated them, as they then make mistakes themselves, the same God of mercy and justice will forgive them if they too repent.

I recently received a letter from a good Latter-day Saint brother. He stated that he had served as a soldier during a war. As they were clearing an area of the enemy, he kicked down the front door of a house while another soldier sprang inside and opened fire with a spray of bullets around the room. Our friend ran upstairs, kicked down a bedroom door, heard a muffled sound behind a closet door, and sprayed the closet with gunfire. He opened the closet door to find that three small children lay lifeless. This experience has tormented him through the years.

Years later his own preteen daughter was living in the home of his best friend. Now the daughter is grown up, has married, and has children of her own. She recently told her father that during the time she lived in his best friend's home, the friend violated her many times. On learning this her father was livid with anger and wanted revenge. The daughter said, "I dared not tell you when I was young; I was fearful you would have killed him!" This man wrote to me in agony, for he had heard me discuss justice "according to the supreme goodness of God." How could he ever forgive his former best friend? As I read the letter and felt the anger and hurt over what his friend had done, I thought about his own tragedy of taking the lives of three innocent little children.

25

The Lord said, "Blessed are the merciful: for they shall obtain mercy" (Matthew 5:7). We must forgive others their trespasses if we would be forgiven ourselves. Justice demands that things be not left undone. Mercy would make certain that justice would do that, for the sake of the innocent.

All of us, including our youth, should seek a deep and abiding understanding of justice. The youth will come to love it and appreciate its purpose. Most understand the need for mercy, but when we come to know the condescension of God, we will express gratitude in beautiful and everlasting praise for the provision He has made in the great plan of happiness for justice and mercy to abide.

5

Joy Unspeakable

God desires that we have joy. Joy is deep and abiding and must be earned. A righteous life brings unspeakable joy. Some will find pleasure in sin but no joy! There are, however, consequences for sin, including sadness, despair, and other dark feelings. Such consequences are unavoidable—sin cannot be covered up and hidden away from God. The Master of heaven and earth is the author of all truth: "Truth is light, and whatsoever is light is Spirit, even the Spirit of Jesus Christ" (D&C 84:45). His commandments are eternal and His ways are just. His prophets and apostles are sure. Their calling is divine, as it has been in days past.

Our understanding is increased and the truths ring clear in the counsel Alma gives to Corianton: "Thou didst do that which was grievous unto me; for thou didst forsake the ministry, and go over into the land of Siron . . . after the harlot Isabel. Yea, she did steal away the hearts of many; but this was no excuse for thee, my son. Thou shouldst have tended to the ministry wherewith thou wast entrusted. Know ye not, my son, that these things are an abomination in the sight of the Lord; yea, most abominable above all sins save it be the shedding of innocent blood or denying the Holy Ghost?" (Alma 39:3–5).

Then with the tenderness of a faithful parent, he exclaimed: "I would not dwell upon your crimes, to harrow up your soul, if it were not for your own good. . . . Now my son, I would that ye should repent and forsake your sins, and go no more after the lusts of your eyes" (verses 7, 9).

And then Alma urges through firm and strong counsel: "Suffer not yourself to be led away by any vain or foolish thing; suffer not the devil to lead away your heart again after those wicked harlots. Behold, O my son, how great iniquity ye brought upon the Zoramites; for when they saw your conduct they would not believe in my words" (verse 11). And a powerful summary word of counsel and perhaps warning: "Wickedness never was happiness" (Alma 41:10).

There are some who think obedience is hard. They think of it as a demand or set of rules forced on them against their will. Some feel that it implies a loss of agency. On the contrary, obedience is a privilege and the only way we can truly be free to progress in the kingdom of God. We ought to get down on our knees and thank God from the innermost part of our souls for the principle of obedience.

Abraham 4:18 states, "And the Gods watched those things which they had ordered until they obeyed." I believe this implies that all will be damned (that is, held back) until they obey—and *all* truly means *all*.

Consider the joy that comes to those who are obedient. Our son Joseph and his family were at a local recreational area. My wife, Merlene, was waiting for them to finish the ride they were taking. Nearby a Hispanic woman seemed to be having a problem. Merlene went to see if she could help. As she assisted the woman, she said, "Are you from Mexico?" The woman replied that she was from Ecuador. Merlene became excited and told her that one of our sons had served a mission for the Church in Ecuador. This woman then stated that she was a convert to the Church and, in broken English, said, "I have been searching for my beloved missionary, the one who converted me. I will always remember and love the missionary who taught and baptized me. His name is Joseph Featherstone." Merlene began to weep and said, "He is our son."

About that time our son, now down from the slide, came over to his mother. As he noticed this woman from Ecuador, there was a moment of recognition, and then, with sweeping emotion, they ran and gave each other a holy hug. Oh, the joy that comes from obedience! Our son didn't have to go on a mission; he did it out of obedience and love for his

Savior. I'm sure he considers his whole mission worth the joy of that one moment with the woman from Ecuador! Sometimes it is difficult and takes great character to be obedient, but I testify that obedience will—within God's time frame—shower us with peace and blessings.

President Mosese Naeata serves as the mission president in Papua, New Guinea. His life has been beset with trials. When he was twelve his father had some serious health problems. They lived in a village in Samoa. The doctor thought it best if young Mosese's father lived near the ocean. They moved down to the beach and built their *fale*. The family farmed, fished, and raised pigs and chickens. Survival was difficult and demanded a lot of time from every family member old enough to help. They had no fresh water supply. When Mosese Naeata went to school, he carried two empty buckets. Together they held five gallons of water. After school he would fill the buckets and walk home, a distance of one and a half miles. His younger sister carried two jugs to school also and filled them each afternoon to take home. This went on for two years!

When Mosese wanted to go to school at BYU—Hawaii some years later, he needed 100 pounds sterling. His brother worked at a school, and he made 20 pounds a month. He asked the principal to advance him six months' salary (120 pounds.) The principal granted his request. The brother then gave 100 pounds to Mosese and lived for six months on the remainder. Later, when this older brother wanted to be sealed in the temple, Mosese went to work on a construction crew. He worked all summer and earned $600, which was enough for his brother to go to New Zealand and be sealed.

Later when Mosese prepared to leave home for his mission in Tonga, his mother talked to him. She said, "Son, this is all the money we have. Use it on your mission." His mother then handed him the equivalent of 50 cents, and he left for his mission. She knew that the Lord would take care of him.

President Naeata and his wife have taken in several children whose parents could not support them. His sister-in-law's husband abandoned her and their nine children. President Naeata took care of and supported that family. After he was called to be a mission president, he built her an 18' x 24' home with several rooms for the family of ten. He was also helping to support his own children who were attending school at

BYU—Hawaii. What a marvelous, sweet story about one who was obedient and followed God at all costs!

In one stake I talked about "justice according to the supreme goodness of God." I suggested that during my ministry I had spoken about love, charity, forgiveness, and mercy, often leaving justice unaddressed. Then I asked, "Who suffers more—the adulterer or the parents with a wayward son or daughter, the incest victim or the perpetrator, the thief or a cancer victim, the sexual pervert or the quadriplegic?" It is my opinion that sometimes the innocent seem to suffer far, far more than the guilty. Somehow that simply does not seem just.

Then I referred to Alma 12:32, which speaks of justice "according to the supreme goodness of God." Earlier, Alma taught the people of Gideon that the Savior suffered for the afflictions, pains, sicknesses, and infirmities of the people—that is justice (see Alma 7:11–12). After reading this, I stated that the innocent must do the same as the guilty to have the effects of the Atonement wrought in their lives. They must turn their burden over to the Savior and forgive the perpetrator, if there has been one.

After the meeting, a wonderful woman came up to me. She was weeping. She told me that for more than 30 years she had suffered, hated, and wanted revenge. Three men had violated her when she was a little girl. She said, "Tonight I understand. During the meeting I transferred my suffering to the Savior. Then I asked if I could forgive the perpetrators. I know that is a correct principle, and I did it sitting in the meeting tonight." She continued, "For the first time in over 30 years the pain, suffering, and hate is gone, and I understand justice 'according to the supreme goodness of God.'"

About three months later I was in the Washington Temple. A woman walked up to me and said, "Do you remember me?" I said, "I imagine I met you at a stake conference some time." She told me yes and then rehearsed our experience together. I became very tender and asked, "How are you doing?" She responded, "Do you know what I am doing in the temple?" When I asked, she replied, "I am having the vicarious work done for the three men I discussed with you." We both wept.

What a marvelous blessing the Atonement is, not only for the guilty but also for the innocent. Remember that forgiveness does not leave justice undone. It simply transfers it to God, whose perfect judgment will ensure that justice is done. Joy comes from obedience, even for the innocent. And obedience may come in the form of following wise counsel, in this case counsel from the scriptures.

Zella Farr Smith told the following romantic story from the life of President David O. and Sister Emma Ray McKay:

Before they were married, they never spoke of having children or determined the number of children they would have. Each had assumed they would gratefully receive as many choice spirits as God would see fit to give them. It was with joy, therefore, that they awaited the birth of their first child. Ray wore her approaching motherhood with glory and dignity, and when David placed the tiny, dark-haired son in her arms, she rejoiced in her motherhood. Yet, strangely enough, that motherhood nearly brought about their first quarrel.

Like all mothers then, Ray had given birth to her baby at home. They had engaged a nurse, but the first night that the nurse left them alone, David had to go to a meeting. As he started to put his hat and coat on, Ray had thought, "Surely you aren't going to a meeting tonight." As if reading her thoughts David turned, looked at her for a moment, and then said, "Have you forgotten that it is the Sunday School board meeting tonight?"

There was no warmth in her kiss as she bade him good-bye. The closing door awakened the baby. Still upset, she sat and rocked the crying baby while the tears of weakness, frustration, and hurt rolled down her cheeks. As she rocked the baby she seemed again to hear her mother's voice saying, "Don't cry over spilt milk." When she was little, Ray had asked, "If I can't cry before I'm hurt, and I can't cry after I'm hurt, when can I cry?" Her mother had answered, "Don't cry at all. Just take things as they come and do the best you can."

Ray was suddenly ashamed of her pettiness. David had a job to do, and he was doing it the best he could. She had a job to do too, and she would do it without complaint. No matter how long David left her again to act in the service of God, Ray never felt any resentment toward him or toward the Church that occupied so much of his time.

Years later this saintly wife and mother sat in the Tabernacle and listened. The music stopped, and the little lady started from her reverie. She needed to listen carefully now. The speaker rose, and at his side stood David—dear, wonderful David. His eyes caught hers just for a moment as they had done so many times before—a brief reassurance of love and confidence. A hush fell over the audience. The man was speaking now: "It is proposed that we sustain David Oman McKay as prophet, seer, and revelator. All those in favor will make it manifest by raising the right hand." The silence was broken only by the rushing sound of ten thousand hands lifted in a sustaining vote. As she looked at her husband standing before the vast assembly, a phrase from the Bible flashed through her mind, "David, beloved of God." (Zella Farr Smith, *A Romantic Story from the Life of President and Sister David Oman McKay*, pp. 3–5.)

How beautiful and wonderful love can be between two souls who love the Lord more than they love each other. What exquisite joy and rapture come to those who are obedient.

In 1955 Margaret Blair Johnstone wrote an article in which she stated: "Love for another person often releases previously unknown emotional power. I shall never forget a man who lived on our street when I was a child. One day I heard the neighborhood gang hoot as he went down the sidewalk with his son's red wagon piled high with wash. 'Hey kid, look at the washer man!' one boy shouted. At that our screen door slammed and my father crossed over to them. I could not hear what he said, but there was no argument as they walked away. I do know what my father said to me, however. 'The bravest man in this neighborhood is John Carr. He has to work at home. His wife will never be well again, there's no one to take care of the baby, and the other children have to go to school. John is doing honest, needed work. Someday he will have a big business; wait and see.' And he did" (*Reader's Digest*, August 1955, p. 178).

It is best that we not judge others; only God knows the heart. Some suffer in silence, some endure beyond belief, some continue on when all hope seems lost, some wither in loneliness. Imagine the ache God must feel for those who suffer and bear it well. As a hen gathereth her chicks under her wings, so the innocent will be embraced in His love and comfort. There will be compensating blessings for every particle of suffering the righteous go through. That would only be just, according to the supreme goodness of God. Joy truly can be indescribable.

For the Church's sesquicentennial year I wanted to share with my children and grandchildren something that has provided me with incredible pleasure, joy, and understanding and is beyond all worldly wealth to me. I wrote a poem entitled "Mormon's Book," which is included in another of my books. It expresses how I feel about the Book of Mormon. There is no amount of money that could purchase from me the influence of this magnificent book. With Ammon I say: "But behold, my joy is full, yea, my heart is brim with joy, and I will rejoice in my God" (Alma 26.11). "Yea, we have reason to praise him forever. . . . Therefore, let us glory, yea, we will glory in the Lord; yea, we will rejoice, for our joy is full; yea, we will praise our God forever. Behold, who can glory too much in the Lord?" (verses 14, 16). "Yea, blessed is the name of my God" (verse 36). "My joy is carried away, even unto boasting in my God; for He has all power, all wisdom, and all understanding" (verse 35).

We receive all this because we have chosen the wonderful privilege of being obedient. The Revelator shares the conditions of those who are obedient: "And I saw a new heaven and a new earth. . . . And I John saw the holy city, new Jerusalem, coming down from God out of heaven. . . . And I heard a great voice out of heaven saying, Behold, the tabernacle of God is with men, and he will dwell with them, and they shall be his people, and God himself shall be with them, and be their God. And God shall wipe away all tears from their eyes; and there shall be no more death, neither sorrow, nor crying, neither shall there be any more pain: for the former things are passed away" (Revelation 21:1–4).

I could add, "And they shall be fair as the moon, and their joy will be full forever and forever." Such is my prayer for all of us.

PART

2

....

LEADING
IN PRINCIPLE

The Deepest Convictions
of Your Life

Several years ago I read about a baccalaureate address given at a major university in America. The speaker suggested that the students take two minutes and consider the deepest convictions of their lives. His address was published in *Vital Speeches*. I have thought about how most students in that particular class would likely have answered the question: "I want a husband or wife who loves me, a family, a nice home, a good job, a good reputation, and plenty of recreation time with my family." Of course, the specifics for each student would vary according to such characteristics as religion, wealth, talents, and the like.

I would like to alter this speaker's request slightly. If you want to have an insightful and generally faith-building response, ask your youth to respond sincerely to this question, whether it be in sacrament meeting, quorum meeting, seminary or other class, or family home evening: "Tell me in a minute or two the deepest convictions of your life; the things that you know more surely than anything else in this world."

At a regional priesthood meeting I invited President John Galanos, president of the Melbourne Australia Maroondah Stake, to come to the pulpit and stand by me. Then I asked him to respond to the above request. A wonderful thing happened. As he attempted to speak, a deep, sweet emotion swept over this wonderful leader. Tears glistened, and he stood deeply moved, unable to utter a word. As I watched, I thought about Ammon's tender feelings: "Behold, my joy is full, yea, my heart is brim with joy, and I will rejoice in my God" (Alma 26:11).

After a minute or two, President Galanos gestured, lifting both hands up in a physical suggestion that the response that came to his mind was so sweet and powerful that words were not available, nor could he bring his emotions sufficiently under control to respond. I said to the priesthood leaders present, "We have had an eloquent, wonderful, spiritual witness of what President Galanos is thinking!" I believe every priesthood leader knew exactly what President Galanos was thinking.

Generally, for those who have a personal witness of this work and who have studied the gospel plan, the response goes something like this: "I know more than I know anything else in this world that there is a God in heaven; that Jesus Christ is literally, physically, the Only Begotten Son of God. I know absolutely that the Book of Mormon is true and that Joseph Smith was a living prophet, apostle, revelator, and seer of God. As much as I know anything, I have a conviction that there are sealing powers on the earth and that my wife and I, and our children, have been sealed for eternity. There is a conviction in my soul, uncompromising, that The Church of Jesus Christ of Latter-day Saints is the only true and living church on this earth. There is a modern prophet who stands at the head of the Church. I know that the Atonement and the Redemption of Christ is an absolute fact and that he is the Savior and the Redeemer of the world. Prayers are answered by a loving Father, and justice and mercy can and will be extended to all who qualify."

Is it any wonder that President Galanos had a difficult time in responding to my request?

As you ask young men and women to sincerely respond, you will learn a great deal about the depth of their testimonies. Quite often I ask persons whom I am interviewing for a restoration of blessings to respond to this request. Very often, quite like President Galanos, when they try to describe their feelings for the Savior and his Atonement, they are overcome with emotion.

Stake presidents and bishops would be wise to cover this issue with young men who have been called on missions. Most will be deeply humbled, and a few will say, "I want to learn while I am on my mission. I want to improve myself and work hard. I would like to be a good companion, and I would like to have a good mission." Of course, these are all worthy desires, but they lack the depth of knowledge needed to be fully motivated by faith in Christ, which is the supreme motivator.

Generally, almost everyone I put this request to starts out with "I know there is a God in heaven who loves me." Isn't that marvelous, that most Latter-day Saints have that witness and that knowledge?

Job declared, "I know that my redeemer liveth, and that he shall stand at the latter day upon the earth: and though after my skin worms destroy this body, yet in my flesh shall I see God: whom I shall see for myself, and mine eyes shall behold, and not another; though my reins be consumed within me" (Job 19:25–27).

And then we read the moving words of Alma: "O that I were an angel, and could have the wish of mine heart, that I might go forth and speak with the trump of God, with a voice to shake the earth, and cry repentance unto every people!" (Alma 29:1).

And Joshua declared, with great power: "If it seem evil unto you to serve the Lord, choose you this day whom ye will serve; whether the gods which your fathers served that were on the other side of the flood, or the gods of the Amorites, in whose land ye dwell: but as for me and my house, we will serve the Lord" (Joshua 24:15).

And in the latter days came this stirring testimony from Joseph Smith and Sydney Rigdon: "And now, after the many testimonies which have been given of him, this is the testimony, last of all, which we give of him: That he lives! For we saw him, even on the right hand of God; and we heard the voice bearing record that he is the Only Begotten of the Father—that by him, and through him, and of him, the worlds are and were created, and the inhabitants thereof are begotten sons and daughters unto God" (D&C 76:22–24).

These are powerful witnesses of those who have convictions that persuade people to believe. Our true convictions determine what our commitment will be. Can you imagine a greater companion in declaring the truth than President John Galanos? With his convictions so deep and wonderful that they are inexpressible, you know what his commitment must be.

Youth need to be around people who have deep convictions. Our convictions direct our lives away from things that are destructive, away from voices that cry out against leaders, the Church, or the doctrine. Having firm convictions about the living God, the atoning Christ, and the power of the Holy Ghost will keep us holding firmly to the iron rod of God.

Elder Sterling W. Sill quoted a poem that our youth need to understand:

> It was such a little little sin
> and such a great big day
> That I thought the hours would swallow it
> or the wind blow it away.
> But the hours passed so quickly by
> and the wind died out somehow
> And the sin that was a weakling then
> is a hungry giant now.
> (*Leadership* [Salt Lake City: Bookcraft, 1958], p. 3).

Those whose convictions are slippery or not firmly in place are in jeopardy because they will have a tendency to compromise some teachings or principles. Firm convictions bring firm commitment.

If you are reading this book, you are probably working in some way with youth. It behooves you to respond to this crucial request: "In a minute or two, describe the deepest convictions of your life—the things you know more than you know anything else in this world." When our convictions are deep enough, God will entrust us to work with his precious youth to bring them safely through.

President Hugh B. Brown, who many years ago served in the Quorum of the Twelve and the First Presidency, said that if he could have chosen any time in the history of the world to be born, he would have chosen to be born about 50 years later. I was born about 50 years later than he was. I have since thought about his desire and wondered when I would have chosen to be born. I would like to have been at the Sweetwater River as an 18-year-old man to help carry the nearly frozen members of a handcart company across those ice-filled, bitterly cold waters. I would also like to live a little further into the 21st century than I am going to. I want to be here when the Church needs defending, for I would be willing to lay my all on the altar for it. Despite these thoughts, after a great deal of pondering, I finally decided I would rather live during this present time than any other. Though I will not be required to wade through icy waters, our generation will be expected to carry the next generation of youth across symbolic rivers of open sewage. Such rivers flow with alcohol, drugs, abortion, homosexual conduct, pedophilia, incest, rape, and every possible perversion.

If we can carry this generation across filthy streams and rivers and hand them over clean and sweet and pure on the far side, we will have prepared the millennial generation for the coming of Christ.

Let the Temple Touch Our Youth

Several years ago the Primary had a program in which children within a reasonable distance of a temple were invited to go to that temple and touch it. Picture a Primary child walking over to a temple wall, reaching reverently out with a small hand, and placing it gently on the wall of that sacred edifice. If properly prepared, most children would find it a wonderful, spiritual experience.

However, some children and youth were not close to a temple. In that case, a teacher would pass around a large picture of a temple so that each child could lay his or her hand on the picture of the temple. Then a discussion would follow about what they felt about the temple as they touched the picture. Of course, with our beloved President Gordon B. Hinckley's vision of temples, in time there *will* be one close enough that every member of the Church can go and actually touch a temple. (Touching a temple need not be for a Primary class alone. For example, it could be a memorable experience for a family home evening.)

Consider what a wise teacher might say to children about touching the temple. He or she might describe how beautiful the temple is inside and explain that this is the place where families are sealed together for eternity. It is the Savior's holy house. At the temple, a teacher might have the children stand back and read the sacred words "Holiness to the

Lord." Then imagine explaining to a child that he or she is a temple of God. We would not defile a temple that we have dedicated to God. Similarly, we should not defile our bodies, which are living temples. Some people smoke, drink alcohol, get involved in drugs, or abuse themselves with tattoos or body piercings, including earrings for young men. All of these things defile our bodies, which are temples.

Imagine what a powerful teaching moment in the life of a child touching the temple could be! But I would like to turn the statement around. What if we let the temple touch us? Teenagers could benefit from asking themselves that question. When a temple touches us, we cannot stay the same—we become better. Once a temple touches us, we will *want* to be better.

There is a beautiful statement on the wall of the matron's office in the Washington Temple, a statement made by President Kimball at the temple dedication. It reads:

> Enter this door as if the floor were gold and every wall of jewels,
> all of wealth untold; as if a choir in robes of fire were singing here.
> Nor shout—nor rush—but hush, for God is here.

In working with our youth, we often do not use all the tools available in our toolbox. We have so many wonderful resources if we would only use them. The temple is one of these special resources. When our youth go to the temple to do baptisms for the dead, they can let the temple touch them.

A young man who was almost 19 was preparing for his mission. He had arranged to spend two months with his parents, who lived in a distant land on a Church assignment. There was a temple nearby. While visiting, he did not have enough time to get a job, so he was left with quite a bit of free time. He went to the temple regularly. The temple president asked if he would like to be an officiator in the temple. You can imagine this young man's excitement. The president assigned him appropriate tasks, and he spent nearly two months in this wonderful calling. He came to love the temple with all his heart. He began to understand the doctrine and teachings of temple worship and service. His desire for spiritual things increased, so he was not so occupied with fads or trends. He simply grew in spiritual stature. To this day that was one of the most spiritually profound opportunities of his life.

How I wish that every worthy 18-year-old young man and woman could have this opportunity. It would change their lives. It would be a tremendous preparation for a mission and marriage. Although in reality the idea is impractical—too many variables to work out—the idea of letting a temple touch us is a true principle.

I remember hearing President Harold B. Lee speak on faith at, I believe, a devotional at Brigham Young University. In essence I believe that he said he had been assigned to a stake conference of one of the stakes in Manti. After the Saturday evening leadership meeting, he and the stake president went out to the car. It had been snowing during the meeting. As I recall the story, there were several inches of snow on the ground. They climbed into the car and drove to the stake president's home. The stake president parked the car in front of the house and turned off the engine. It was snowing heavily. Two blocks up the street was the beautiful Manti Temple. The temple is white, the lights were white, and the snowstorm was beautiful. They watched for a long moment, and then the stake president turned and said: "Elder Lee, the temple is never more beautiful than in times of storm." What a marvelous thought with a multitude of applications!

President Hunter put things in proper perspective when he taught, "Let us prepare every missionary to go to the temple worthily, and make that experience an even greater highlight than receiving the mission call." In the same talk he made some other statements about the temple that are significant:

"The things that we must do and not do to be worthy of a temple recommend are the things that ensure that we will be happy as individuals and as families.

"Let us truly be a temple-attending and a temple-loving people. . . . We should not go only for our kindred dead, but also for the personal blessings of temple worship, for the sanctity and the safety that are within those hallowed and consecrated walls. As we attend the temple, we learn more richly and deeply the purpose of life and the significance of the atoning sacrifice of the Lord Jesus Christ. Let us make the temple, together with temple worship and temple covenants and temple marriage, our ultimate earthly goal and the supreme mortal experience" (*Ensign,* Feb. 1995, p. 5).

That is quite a description from a prophet of God—"*the supreme mortal experience.*" That is what will happen to our youth if they will let the temple touch them.

During the time we served in the Philippines, a father related a concern in their family. They lived on an island far distant from the temple. Transportation to the temple was expensive. They had four children—three in college and one in high school. The father felt a need to have his family sealed to him and his wife. During family council they discussed the problem—they did not have the money to make the trip to the temple. This condition was not going to change in the near future. After discussion the father said, in essence, "The only way we can go to the temple is to have our three college students drop out of college, our high-school student drop out of school, and all of you work a year to save enough money." They would have to save the tuition and school monies for all four children, and then the four students would have to work for a year to earn enough money in order to go to the temple. The children agreed to drop out of school and work for a year for the privilege of going to the temple. Without any knowledge of what President Hunter would say in the future, they somehow knew that this was "the supreme mortal experience."

Teach our youth that everything we do in the temple ties to the Atonement. This will help our youth desire to understand the Atonement. Most young people, if asked what the Atonement means, will respond, "Through the Atonement we can be forgiven of our sins." Of course, that is correct, but forgiveness comes through repentance, which includes change in behavior, sorrow for the transgression, making restitution if possible, and exercising obedience and faith in the Savior. Most youth do not understand that they will either repent or suffer: "Therefore I command you to repent—repent, lest I smite you by the rod of my mouth, and by my wrath, and by my anger, and your sufferings be sore—how sore you know not, how exquisite you know not, yea, how hard to bear you know not. For behold, I, God, have suffered these things for all, that they might not suffer if they would repent; but if they would not repent they must suffer even as I" (D&C 19:15–17).

If we choose not to repent, then justice demands suffering. This suffering will be exquisite and, until they go to the temple, youth may understand neither the marvelous blessings that come from repenting nor the dread consequences if they choose not to repent.

Our youth need to be taught about the temple so they will begin to understand God's divine role for women and for men. The temple teaches men how to treat women. We hear of a great number of young men who date girls and then physically abuse them as if they had some right to do whatever they wanted. Interestingly, Elder B. H. Roberts said, "Men who are fiercest with other men are gentlest with women" (Truman G. Madsen, *Defender of the Faith* [Salt Lake City: Bookcraft, 1980], p. 96). And I would add, "Men who beat upon women or girls are cowardly when facing real men." The temple leads men to treat women with dignity, softness, kindness, and love. A man with any other attitude is not worthy of a temple recommend.

While in the Philippines I was in my office one day when I saw a woman crossing the street walking on her knees, dragging her two little crippled legs. She had a sister holding one hand and another holding the other. She must have had terribly calloused knees. They went into the temple. I called Bishop Santos in our Welfare Department and asked him how long it would take him to buy a wheelchair and take it to the temple. He thought he could do it in an hour or so. I asked him to buy one and take it to the temple. Then I said, "Wait there and a woman will come out walking on her knees. Please present it to her."

He bought the wheelchair, took it to the temple, and hid it behind a pillar. It was not long until this little lady came out walking on her knees. He said to her, "Do you have a wheelchair?" She said she did not and began to cry, explaining, "I used to have one and it simply wore out and cannot be fixed. I will never be able to afford another one as long as I live. They are too expensive." Bishop Santos gently asked, "How would you like a new wheelchair?" The tears came fast from her, as well as from the sisters assisting her. Bishop Santos went behind the pillar and pulled out the new wheelchair. They lifted her up into it. The tears continued, but now they were tears of gratitude. Bishop Santos could not hold back his tears. Later he said, "President Featherstone, we live in a beautiful and magnificent church."

If our youth could only understand how important the temple is, they too would be willing to "walk on their knees," if necessary, to get to the temple. And what comes of such sacrifice? Horace Cummings recorded that Joseph Smith declared that "those who had been worked for in the temple would fall at the feet, would kiss the feet, would express the most exquisite gratitude, for those who did that work" (as cited in the book commemorating the centennial celebration of the Manti Temple).

In one of our training meetings, Elder Russell M. Nelson referred to the temple recommend as a "badge of courage." Our youth today must become such men and women of courage. We must help them understand and gain a desire to go to the temple. We must teach them that they need to let the temple touch them.

Communicating in the Next Millennium

As we enter the seventh millennium, we usher our youth into the era of greatest evil in the history of the world. In scripture we have been told the conditions of the world just before our Lord and Master's second coming:

"In those days, shall be great tribulation on the Jews, and upon the inhabitants of Jerusalem, such as was not before sent upon Israel, of God, since the beginning of their kingdom until this time; no, nor ever shall be sent again upon Israel. . . .

"For in those days there shall also arise false Christs, and false prophets, and shall show great signs and wonders, insomuch, that, if possible, they shall deceive the very elect, who are the elect according to the covenant. . . .

"And they shall hear of wars, and rumors of wars.

"Behold I speak for mine elect's sake; for nation shall rise against nation, and kingdom against kingdom; there shall be famines, and pestilences, and earthquakes, in divers places.

"And again, because iniquity shall abound, the love of men shall wax cold; but he that shall not be overcome, the same shall be saved. . . .

"And again shall the abomination of desolation, spoken of by Daniel the prophet, be fulfilled. . . .

"Verily, I say unto you, this generation, in which these things shall be shown forth, shall not pass away until all I have told you shall be fulfilled. . . .

"And, as I said before, after the tribulation of those days, and the powers of the heavens shall be shaken, then shall appear the sign of the Son of Man in heaven, and then shall all the tribes of the earth mourn; and they shall see the Son of Man coming in the clouds of heaven, with power and great glory" (Joseph Smith—Matthew 1:18, 22, 28–30, 32, 34, 36).

This gives us a small clue as to how dark and evil conditions will become for our clean, wholesome youth. It will not be a day without casualties. We will see many precious youth succumb to the pleasures and passions offered by the world. One of those might be a passion for communication. Like many passions, when handled appropriately it can be incredibly uplifting and enlightening; however, when abused, communication can invite the spirit of the devil as quickly as any vice available in the world.

For example, language too often used at school, on the streets, and in athletic competitions is so abominable that it literally pains the pure in heart. The offenses are beyond description. We have multicultural language with the most filthy, degrading expressions about things we hold precious and dear. Frequently there is not a twinge of conscience as youth and adults, movie stars and athletes sound off with a chain of filth and profanity.

These things are offensive to those souls in and out of the Church who have a sense of dignity. Our youth and university students are exposed to much of this under the protective umbrella of "free speech."

Think about our youth and the strings of four-letter words, the anti-Christ behavior, the profaning of Deity, and the gutter expressions that have become what they regularly hear as part of their normal day at school. We have racists, fascists, extreme feminists, homosexuals, and pornography peddlers that absolutely glow in the influence they exert on modern society. Even some self-proclaimed intellectuals (and aren't most "intellectuals" self-proclaimed?) stoop to new lows when it comes to encouraging free speech so offensive that even the heavens must surely close against it.

Along with the deepening cesspool of gutter speech is the growth of various forms of harassment, something that will increase in the lives of our active LDS youth and young adults as the polarization of decency and degradation increases.

I love our fair, clean, wholesome youth. They have been preserved for this generation. Who among us will stand and reinforce their standards against the flood of harassing and abusive language, perverted speech, and distorted values?

A giant evil serves to debase all we hold precious and dear. In the name of free speech come the most demeaning and filthy assaults on the center figure of all Christianity—our Lord, Jesus the Christ. The same biased criticism rolls off the tongues of those who demean motherhood and the great armies of Christian women who choose to be wives and mothers, who feel and understand their God-given roles to bear, nurture, train, and rear children. Those who oppose our conservative views loudly blare their prejudices and biases in an attempt to silence anyone with an opposing view. Free speech is wonderful, they say, as long as it does not conflict with their thinking!

Hosts of immoral, dishonest, sexually permissive, perverted homosexuals and pedophiles want to come out into the open to declare their lustful orientation as being acceptable behavior. But they come down like a hammer upon all moral, God-fearing people who espouse *their* beliefs. How do our youth respond to such indignities?

We must stand firm as a great support system. We must prove by example that the most powerful expression in any language is free from slang, profanity, and sexual innuendos. There is a purity and an eloquence that resounds in the statements and phrases of men and women of character and culture. In any language there is sufficient vocabulary to communicate in a decent, appropriate, inoffensive way.

Let us consider the following in all our teaching:

EXAMPLE

As stated above, we teach best when we teach by example. Our home, therefore, is the center of most of our important communicating.

We need to let the youth and children in our homes know that certain language and expressions are unacceptable.

A few years ago our son was in a school choir. The drama and music departments decided to put on a once-popular production entitled *Jesus Christ, Superstar.* I said to our son, "Do you know how referring to our Lord in that way offends my soul?" He was young and inexperienced, but he was enlightened and could reason through what I said. Now there are far more insulting paintings and perverse music that degrades and persecutes our Lord and Master. The terrifying thing is that it is going to get worse. Satan is the archenemy of Jesus Christ. His dark and loathsome mission is to destroy the Son of God and His disciples.

We all know that Lucifer has no ground rules—not a particle of good or a twinge of conscience. He is totally evil, without one redeeming virtue. I cannot comprehend the mind of one who would find pleasure in the sexual violation of innocent children or downplay the consequences of drugs, suicide, abortion, and pornography. How evil and how powerful!

Our examples are critical. Our youth simply must see, feel, and know how purely—and quietly—Latter-day Saints can communicate.

PEER INFLUENCE

Peer influence can be for good or evil. I want our youth to have social experiences with others who have the same standards they do. It is easy to control tongue and thoughts when we are with others who elevate our conduct. There is something glorious and beautiful about wholesome, faith-building experiences with others who have common standards. There is strength in numbers, and there is also security. (Remember the counsel in our chapter on seminary?)

I recently was given a youth's description of her seminary teacher. This description was in the history of a seminary class of some years ago: "Our teacher—not only for this year but for the rest of our lives! This man is so many things that no words can be written to accurately describe him. A teacher of leaders; a man of compassion and understanding; a friend of everyone lucky enough to meet him. He teaches of the Savior by living a Christlike life himself. During this year every member of our class grew to love and lean on this man. He is aware of the problems that face us today. He actually gets involved in whatever his students are involved in—school, football games, music concerts, plays, dances, or church parties. He takes note of whatever we accomplish. Brother —— will be remembered for teaching us to live. He taught us how to gain spiritual uplift from everyday happenings and how to appreciate those around us. The graduated class will long remember Brother —— and the privilege they had to sit among the lucky members of his class."

This sweet, young historian concludes her history thus: "At the beginning of the year, Brother —— vowed to try to make each day a spiritual experience. For each of us he succeeded. He made going to seminary a spiritual experience and a worthwhile endeavor. Going to school was much easier after spending the morning studying the Lord."

TRAINING AND TEACHING

It is imperative that our children be taught and trained how to communicate. President David O. McKay stated: "There is no greater responsibility in this world than the training of a human soul." The home is where we do this best. Children express themselves much the way their parents do. They develop tender feelings from listening to their parents' expressions. For example, my wife and I easily shed tears when we are humbled or filled with the Spirit. All seven of our children seem to weep easily and have special, tender feelings for things of the Spirit.

Several years ago I sat in a meeting in the Salt Lake Temple with other General Authorities. President N. Eldon Tanner took a few minutes and trained us to pronounce often-used words correctly. Such words included *Golgotha, err,* and several others that are commonly mispronounced. So should we correct our children lovingly, teaching the benefits of better communicating in their everyday lives.

RESISTANCE TO INAPPROPRIATE LANGUAGE

Our youth may hear four-letter words and evil, perverted phrases, but they don't need to listen to them or let them penetrate into their vocabulary. All of us have been through the process of controlling our speech. Teach them what you do to not contaminate your mind with mental garbage and expressions.

When our youth have a language style of their own, they will begin to exercise an influence for decency. Those who speak with a good, clean vocabulary will become fewer and fewer in our society, as a rule. They will rise to influential heights because they are different. In fact, I predict that simply having an *attitude* of resisting the trend toward degrading and uncouth speech will make a major difference in their lives and conduct.

SPIRITUAL AND SCRIPTURAL REINFORCEMENT

I have long believed that spiritual experiences have a great influence on our conduct. Not long ago I talked to a stake president who came to a meeting that required of him four hours of driving time to the meeting and four hours back home. Great were the spiritual rewards to all in attendance. He later said, "If it had required twelve hours each way I would not have missed that meeting!"

When President Boyd K. Packer came to our area training, he asked and answered questions, taught as a master teacher, and spoke as a seer and revelator. After the nearly eight-hour meeting had concluded, he went to the back door to shake hands with the stake presidents, temple president, and mission presidents as they were leaving. They did not want to leave. He quietly commented, "Do you feel what is happening?" I did, because I was feeling the same thing. I didn't want to lose the spirit I had felt all day long.

When our youth have spiritual experiences, they build strength. They come to understand what a grand and glorious feeling it is to have the Spirit with them and do not want to lose it. Remember, the Spirit is very, very sensitive. It will withdraw from us if we offend it by using inappropriate language, thinking unholy thoughts, or doing things we should not. The Spirit will leave us when we "walk where angels fear to tread."

The interesting thing about the Spirit when it withdraws is that it does not come back immediately after we have finished telling the unclean joke or have left the movie theater where we watched a crude or degrading movie. If we have driven the Spirit away, we have to repent and sincerely crave the return of the Spirit and its influence in our lives. Then, after a period of regaining worthiness and humbling ourselves, we will again feel the peace that comes from having the Spirit abide in us.

The second part of working to have frequent spiritual experiences involves our study of the scriptures. Studying the scriptures puts our youth in touch with the noblest thoughts of the best men who ever lived. It opens and enlightens our minds to great concepts as far reaching as God and His eternities. President Packer has stated that studying the doctrines of the gospel changes behavior more quickly than a study of behavior changes behavior. The root of that doctrinal study is regular immersion in the scriptures.

Understanding the Atonement and the love and life of our Master, the Son of God, will cause our youth to love and worship Him. Those who know Him will not want to offend Him. The sixth beatitude is "Blessed are the pure in heart: for they shall see God" (Matthew 5:8). In 3 Nephi 12:8, the Lord teaches the same principle. I believe the Savior spoke truly and meant the statement literally. I also believe that we can see God and His majesty in many ways. At general conference I see the majesty of God through his anointed leaders. I see God in the wonderful acts of kindness that his disciples here on earth perform—caring for the poor, the widow, the sick, and the abused, and performing a thousand quiet deeds for good. Our youth, once they have feasted on the Spirit, will not want to lose it.

Of course, there are many diverse paths and methods for avoiding worldly communications. We have only discussed a few. As I have worked on each chapter of this book, I have thought of the spiraling downward of morals and standards, language and conduct. Unfortunately, we have not yet bottomed out, nor will we for some years ahead, when the Holy One of Israel will come as King of kings and Lord of lords.

We can, however, preserve a righteous generation to await and prepare for his Second Coming. There will be a generation of youth "fair as the sun, and clear as the moon" (D&C 105:31), but it will take the greatest effort by all of us who work with youth—parents, bishops, advisers, home teachers, Scout and activity leaders, Sunday School and Primary teachers. Remember, success in a calling requires a testimony, training, time, and tenure. I know God will bless our efforts, which will result in the fairest generation of all time.

"Men without Chests"

Author C. S. Lewis portrays an interesting concept with his phrase "men without chests"—that is, people without moral courage. I believe that we live in a generation of this type of people. It is an interesting experience to ask the young men in any Aaronic Priesthood quorum what this phrase means to them. If you do, you will hear a lot of very good answers and some questionable ones, but the exercise will usually be worth it.

We even have great athletes without chests. And there are teachers and coaches who have great influence yet lack chests. A few years ago I was told of a woman who coached a girls' basketball team in Wyoming: she wanted to win in such a way that it "humbled" her opponents, who were a very poor team. I have forgotten the score, but it was something like 80–5. This coach had her team press full court from the tipoff to the final second of the game. Can you imagine a woman who coaches young women to have no more sense than the empty ball they were dribbling?

A football coach whose team was playing the Golden Owls sprayed a chicken with gold paint and then had his players stomp it to death! Another coach whose team was about to play against the Texas Longhorns had his team watch while a Texas longhorn bull was castrated! What price do we pay to win?

I did hear of a marvelous example of a team that won their division championship but, on reviewing the game video and realizing that they had had 12 players on the field, they relinquished the trophy! What a contrast to coaches without chests.

An assistant coach of a football team walked over to a young man on the team. The coach spit out a tirade of profanity and then smashed his forearm into the throat of the player. It knocked him down, and for a few moments he couldn't breathe. The father of the young man said afterward that he wanted to say to the coach, "I think there is a better, more manly way of correcting a mistake than for a grown man to smash his forearm into the throat of a young player!" and then mete back to the coach what he had done to his son. Of course, he didn't do it, which is what the Savior would expect from all of us. But the father said it was a great temptation.

Sometimes we even have political and religious leaders who do not have chests. Consider the blatant immorality that sometimes occurs at the highest levels of government. Our youth are exposed to constant media attention on these matters, which focuses on the number of people who prefer to overlook immorality. Two major evangelists, known worldwide, are known to have violated codes of morality and honesty. One of these went to prison. I watched the news when the other one admitted his involvement with a prostitute and cried large tears of sorrow for the television viewers. He asked for forgiveness and seemed deeply repentant. However, within a year or two he was again involved sexually with another woman.

These are examples, I believe, of "men without chests." As a Church we are in a predicament: few outside the Church can become true heroes and heroines to our youth. Only occasionally do we hear of someone who really does care for the youth and has lifetime goals of serving a special generation of students.

The following poem I composed as I was writing this chapter. It may sound negative—and it is. It is true outside the Church, but thank God it is not true inside this wonderful Church of men *with* chests, and women with great hearts and hands to help.

"Men without Chests"

Mighty men and valiant
And strong and brave and true

Did many monumental things
That few on earth will do.
They conquered giant mountains
And rode the storm-tossed seas;
They searched the deepest ocean floors
And logged the tallest trees.
They trod with strides of giants
From pole to pole and back.
They tackled unknown depths in space
And northern polar pack.
They rode across the seven seas
And faced great dangers there.
The greatest of them all have claimed
They gained their strength through prayer.
These were the great and noble,
The ones with chests of men.
Oh, how we need such mighty ones
To do such deeds again!

But now we see the saddening truth—
We no more top the crests
But bear the mediocrity
Of men who have no chests.
In shame we watch the actions
Of those we once could trust—
Who compromise their honesty
And gratify their lust.
Oh, shameless generation
Of men who have no chests,
You could have worked in grandeur
You could have been the best.
But this great truth will ring through time
And shackle us with shame:
We labored in a day of men
Who knew no hero's fame.

One of my favorite writers has, over the years, published several talks in *Vital Speeches of the Day*. His name is Kenneth Jernigen. He was the former president of the National Federation of the Blind. He is blind himself and is one of those in our day who qualifies as a man "with a chest." I want to share with you something he said at a convention for the blind in New Orleans. The principle he espouses is a wonderful one for those who have been greatly wronged in the past and who feel a need for reparation or vindication:

"Let me be specific. If a blind person tries to exploit blindness to get an advantage, or tries to use blindness as an excuse for failure or bad behavior, we must not defend that blind person, but we must stand with the sighted person that the blind person is trying to victimize. This will not be easy; it will not always be politically correct; and it will frequently bring criticism, not only from those blind persons who claim to want equality but are not willing to earn it, but from some of the sighted as well. But we must do it anyway. If we want equal treatment and true integration, we must act like equals and not hide behind minority statutes. Yes, blind people are our brothers and sisters, but so are the sighted. Unless we are willing to have it that way we neither deserve, nor truly want, what we have always claimed as a 'birthright.' We are capable of working with the sighted, playing with the sighted, and living with the sighted, and we are capable of doing it on terms of complete equality. Likewise, the sighted are capable of doing the same with us and, for the most part, want to. What we need is not confrontation but understanding, and understanding that runs both ways" (*Vital Speeches,* Aug. 15, 1997, p. 645).

I am impressed with this healthy, refreshing attitude! There indeed is a man with a chest so big and broad that he is influencing a whole generation of blind and sighted people in understanding and working toward equality.

There are some things indispensable in men with chests and women with helping hands and hearts. They teach our youth that integrity, character, loyalty, humility, hard work, ambition, trustworthiness, kindness, compassion, spirituality, and commitment are traits of quality men and women. They are the fibre of the substance of which we should be made.

It is my belief that God continues to bless our youth with the ability to see the difference between quality individuals and those with lesser light. I love the term *ramrod straight.* It describes those who are completely committed to the gospel.

This chapter is written to help our youth discern between men with and without chests. I remember the first time I read C. S. Lewis's statement about men without chests. I could see as clearly as on a screen a whole generation of arrogant, proud, and discontented athletes; flirtatious and unfaithful men in business; dishonest laborers who would steal tools and equipment; unworthy college students cheating on exams; and many other such images. Contrast all of these with our First Presidency, the Twelve Apostles, and faithful stake presidents and bishops. These are men of substance and value.

Of course, the supreme example of heaven and earth is the Lord, our Redeemer. Let us all teach our youth that He is the true exemplar and will be forever and ever.

God Pains with Their Tears

The Savior, with loving compassion, blessed the little children on his visit to his "other sheep" on the American continent: "And when he had said these words, he wept, and the multitude bare record of it, and he took their little children, one by one, and blessed them, and prayed unto the Father for them. And when he had done this he wept again" (3 Nephi 17:21–22).

I find myself wondering if, among other reasons, He wasn't weeping for all the innocent children who suffer tragic indignities. Oh, what a blessing it would be for every innocent child who would ever walk the earth to be blessed individually by the Savior. From experience we know they will not have that blessing on this side of the veil, but in our homes righteous fathers can exercise their priesthood to call down His blessings on His little ones.

When our family was young we had an alcoholic father, and he was the only member of the Church in our family. When we were old enough, with Mother's permission, we joined the Church. After Mom and Dad were divorced, with no alimony or child support, there were times when conditions at home were pretty sparse. Sometimes we had little food. It seemed that each time this happened, Bishop Percy Schofield always showed up after dark and brought food. To my knowledge, no one outside the family knew of our need, but it seemed the bishop did know, and he assisted us.

There could have been some in the ward who might have legitimately said, "Don't baptize the Featherstone children into the Church. You will just be baptizing another welfare family." Well, that was true to some extent. The bishop had brought food from time to time. And as we children became older, I worked at the cannery and on other welfare projects to help earn what had been given, as did my brothers.

On a plaque on the Statue of Liberty are these words, penned by Emma Lazarus:

> Not like the brazen giant of Greek fame
> With conquering limbs astride from land to land
> Here at our sea washed sunset gates shall stand
> A mighty woman with a torch whose flame
> Is the imprisoned lightning and her name
> Mother of Exiles. Her Beacon hand glows
> Worldwide welcome. Her mild eyes command
> The air bridged harbor that twin cities frame.
> Keep ancient lands your storied pomp, cries she with silent lips,
> Give me your tired, your poor, your huddled masses
> Yearning to breathe free, the wretched refuse of your
> Teeming shore.
> Send these the homeless tempest tossed to me.
> I lift my lamp beside the golden door.

Well, I am not quite certain, as wonderful as this nation is, that we can still honor that invitation. But this Church can. "Give [us] your tired, your poor, your huddled masses yearning to breathe free, the wretched refuse of your teeming shore. Send these the homeless tempest tossed to [us]. [We] lift [our] lamp beside the golden door." The gospel is the golden door. I thank God every day of my life for what this magnificent Church means to each one of us in our family. It has been the guiding force in my life since those early days of need with Bishop Schofield. I have thought often of those days and, as a result, our contributions to the Church have always been generous. Though we have been blessed to repay many times over whatever we might have received when we were among the tired and poor, the greatest blessings have come from the peace and family relationships resulting from following our Savior in His Church.

Just a couple of years before my mother and father were divorced, when I was about 11 years old, Mother was working at Garfield Smelter, like a man. She needed those wages to support us. She would wear overalls, a flannel shirt, and men's logger boots with metal toes to protect her feet. She quite often worked the graveyard shift. She would come home from work and get us children up for school; then she would fix breakfast. When we came home for lunch, she was up. When we came home after school, she was up. She took care of the six or seven children at the time, prepared all the meals, and did the housework, the washing, and the ironing.

One Saturday morning she came home from work, slept a couple of hours, got up, and began to clean the house and prepare a meal for all her relatives on her side of the family. There must have been 35 or 40 with our own family. She worked all day making biscuits, preparing a roast with all the trimmings, baking cakes and pies, and putting up the tables and setting them. At about 6:00 P.M. the family all showed up. We had a wonderful dinner. Then everyone stacked the dirty dishes, took them into the kitchen, and placed them on the drain boards. They brought all of the leftover food and put it on the counters, took down the tables, closed the kitchen door, and began to visit. By this time it was about 8:00 P.M. I remember I was standing all alone in the kitchen. I looked at all the dirty dishes, silverware, pots, pans, and all the food still on the counter. I remember thinking, "This isn't fair. My mother worked all night long at Garfield Smelter, she only had a couple of hours sleep, she has worked all day preparing this meal, and when everyone leaves she will have all these dishes to do. Everyone will leave about 11:00 P.M., and my mother will have to stay up until about 2:00 A.M. to wash the dishes and clean up the kitchen. That isn't fair!"

As I stood there I suddenly thought, "I will do the dishes." I filled the sink with hot water, for there were no electric dishwashers in those days—I was it! I washed the dishes, batch after batch, changing the dishwater often; batch after batch, I rinsed them off and dried them. I had an old bakery apron on. It hung almost to the floor on me. It was soaking wet. I changed the water again and did all the silverware, then changed it again for the glasses and crystal. Last of all I did the pots and pans. I learned a great lesson—if you wash pots and pans as soon as you finish using them when the food is still soft, they are easier to clean; don't wait until the food hardens and dries. I scrubbed and scrubbed until finally all the dishes were done. I put the food away in the ice-a-box (in our family, we claim that's Italian for *refrigerator*, except ours really was an ice box), then I cleaned and wiped off all the counters.

By this time there must have been half an inch of water all over the floor. Mother had taught me how to scrub the floor, about a 30-inch section at a time. I scrubbed the entire kitchen floor on my hands and knees. Then I surveyed my work. To my young mind the kitchen looked immaculate. It had taken me just about three hours. Pretty soon I could hear chairs shuffling in the living room as everyone was getting up to leave. I remember standing in the kitchen, soaking wet from head to foot, looking to make sure I had missed nothing. Then I heard the last one leave, and my mom's steps came toward the kitchen. There was a swinging door. She pushed it open and walked in.

I wish I could tell you what happened then, but I don't think I was old enough to understand. But one thing I did recognize was her shock. Then there came another look. I couldn't tell at that time, but as I look back it seems that it was a deep, sweet, look of appreciation, one that said, "Thank you. I think you understand I am very tired, and I love you." She came over and hugged me, and I went to bed with a great love in my heart for our mother who did so much for us.

One Sunday morning the teacher for the Sunbeam class came up to a sweet sister in the Primary presidency and said, "I can't stay to teach my class today. Can you arrange for someone to cover for me? Our lesson is on feelings." Before she left, the teacher put several faces on the blackboard—a happy face, a sad face, and others.

A member of the presidency took over. She had all the little children sit on the floor in front of her and then said, pointing to each face, "What is this?" And the children responded. When she pointed to the happy face, she said, "What is this?" and the children echoed, "It's a happy face." Then she asked each child, "And are you happy?" Everyone said yes—except Sara (not her real name), who said, "No, teacher, I have a broken heart."

Concerned, this kind sister had the little girl come up to her: she knelt on the floor, put her arms around Sara, and said, "Boys and girls, it isn't right for Sara to have a broken heart. Can everyone say something nice about Sara?" One by one the children said nice things about her shoes, her dress, the ribbon in her hair; and they each told her she was pretty. When they finished the teacher said, "Now, Sara, I love you, and all the children love you; doesn't that make you happy?" Sara replied, "No, teacher, my mommy and daddy are getting a divorce, and I have a broken heart!"

When I heard that story I too had a broken heart. This member of the ward Primary presidency went to Sara's home several times after that to take some goodies and to sit and visit with Sara. She said, "I am grateful that I was there to teach the class that day and was able to help Sara. I would not have missed that opportunity for anything."

The First Presidency's proclamation on the family states: "Husband and wife have a solemn responsibility to love and care for each other and for their children. . . . Husbands and wives, mothers and fathers, will be held accountable before God for the discharge of these obligations."

Mark Draper, who was president of the National Education Taskforce, Inc., gave a speech entitled "Shall the Family Endure?" In it he quoted a nationally renowned author who said, "Marriage is one chosen life-style, but before choosing it people should weigh its costs and benefits against other options. Divorce is part of the normal family cycle and is nothing deviant or tragic."

Mr. Draper then responded: "Pardon me—divorce a part of the normal family cycle and nothing deviant or tragic? I don't think so. What *is* deviant and tragic here is that we have such over-educated fools teaching our youngsters such nonsensical trash!"

"Nothing tragic!" Tell Sara that, because she has a broken heart.

In regard to divorce, Mr. Draper further stated: "Women experience a 73 percent decline in their standard of living, while their former husbands experience a 42 percent increase." Then he proceeded with this positive observation: "How many of you believe that half of all marriages end up in divorce? You have been lied to. Here is the actual fact: the number of divorces each year is equal to one half of the number of new marriages. In other words, twice as many people get married each year as get divorced. Enemies of heterosexuality and marriage twist these numbers to suggest that half of all marriages end in divorce, but this is false, as you can see. This is the real statistic to remember—each year fewer than one percent of marriages end in divorce" (*Vital Speeches*, August 15, 1994).

I love what Mormon wrote to his son about little children: "Wherefore, little children are whole, for they are not capable of committing sin. . . . I know that it is solemn mockery before God, that ye should baptize little children. . . . Parents . . . must . . . humble themselves as their little children, and they shall all be saved with their little children" (Moroni 8: 8–10).

As recorded in 3 Nephi, the Savior "did teach and minister unto the children of the multitude of whom hath been spoken, and he did loose their tongues, and they did speak unto their fathers great and marvelous things, even greater than he had revealed unto the people; and he loosed their tongues that they could utter. . . . And they both saw and heard these children; yea, even babes did open their mouths and utter marvelous things; and the things which they did utter were forbidden that there should not any man write them" (3 Nephi 26:14, 16).

I love children and, with you, it breaks my heart to see them hurt or suffering. Although doctrinally there may be only one unforgivable sin, my heart tells me that there are some that must be very close to unforgivable. Imagine the depth of cruelty in the world that drives degenerate men and women to kidnap infants and little children and sell them. I cannot conceive how evil the heart of a person must be to do such a terrible thing without even a twinge of conscience. And woe, woe, woe be to those who abuse little children, sexually or any other way. *How can this happen?*

Thank God for the Atonement that permits every child who suffers innocently to be taught that Jesus knows how much they hurt; He has suffered for them. With one divine caress every terror, horror, and particle of pain can be removed. Through the Atonement, Jesus Christ can remove the burdens of the guilty, and His great love will cover the innocent, especially little children.

I feel so strongly about this that I have written the following verse in an attempt to say poetically what I hold in my heart:

God Pains with Their Tears

How lovely and special our children can be
When they leave Father's presence to join you and me.

As babies the veil is still open wide;
They can't tell about it, while they lie by your side.
But nonetheless it is wonderfully true,
And methinks God watches each little one, too.
Then slowly the veil closes for the rest of their lives,
While the little ones grow and somehow survive.

They learn to walk and more swiftly they grow
But the divinity in them they still seem to know.
They can penetrate deeply the most calloused heart
They can bring you to laughter that tears you apart.
Their soft little fingers and angel-like faces
Are seen in your dreams and a dozen like places.
They thrill you with first words and first steps they take—
Then suddenly one candle on their first birthday cake.

And on through the years they wrap 'round your heart,
And always you fear you'll lose even a part.
At two and at three they bring humor and fun,
At four, five, and six years they shine like the sun.
So while they are children, we all must assure
That they are protected, left clean, sweet, and pure.
For God grants them to us to joy through the years,
But when we offend them, God pains with their tears.

Jacob reminds us in these tender words of offenses to our wives and children: "Yea, it grieveth my soul and causeth me to shrink with shame before the presence of my Maker, that I must testify unto you concerning the wickedness of your hearts. And also it grieveth me that I must use so much boldness of speech concerning you, before your wives and your children, many of whose feelings are exceedingly tender and chaste and delicate before God, which thing is pleasing unto God; and it supposeth me that they have come up hither to hear the pleasing word of God, yea, the word which healeth the wounded soul" (Jacob 2:6–8).

After Jacob spoke of the wrongfulness of their search for gold and silver, the pride of their hearts, their stiff necks and high heads, the costliness of their apparel, their persecuting their brethren—after all this, he then admonished them "to do good—to clothe the naked, and to feed the hungry, and to liberate the captive, and administer relief to the sick and the afflicted" (verse 19).

Unfortunately, Jacob had yet more difficult words to speak: "And now I make an end of speaking unto you concerning this pride. And were it not that I must speak unto you concerning a grosser crime, my heart would rejoice exceedingly because of you. But the word of God burdens me because of your grosser crimes," iniquities that included whoredoms and other sexual improprieties (verses 23–23).

Then Nephi's prophet-brother speaks these words for the Lord: "And I will not suffer, saith the Lord of Hosts, that the cries of the fair daughters of this people, . . . shall come up unto me against the men of my people. . . . For they shall not lead away captive the daughters of my people because of their tenderness. . . . Behold, ye have done greater iniquities than the Lamanites, our brethren. Ye have broken the hearts of your tender wives, and lost the confidence of your children, because of your bad examples before them; and the sobbings of their hearts ascend up to God against you" (verses 32–33, 35).

Now think of our children in homes where they are mistreated, and wives who live under similar conditions: "And because of the strictness of the word of God, which cometh down against you, many hearts died, pierced with deep wounds" (verse 35).

I think that the Savior must be pleased with all of you wonderful parents who love, nurture, joy in, and care tenderly for His little ones. I think mother earth must moan deep within when she sees the offenses to children. God, in his great compassion, wisdom, and justice, will not let one single indignity against his little children be left unaddressed.

Of all the trusts God has given us, the blessing of children may be the greatest. It is a sacred trust. Let us, as a Church, stand as a great, giant, granite pillar against those who oppose or abuse the family.

11

Healing the Scars of Abuse

More of our youth in the Church than we would like to believe have been abused—sexually, physically, and mentally. This chapter was not in my book of 25 years ago. We were not so much aware of the problem at that time. We also live in a day when parents are abused—mostly mentally and emotionally, but some physically. Some of our rebellious youth curse, insult, demean, intimidate, and harass their parents. Hopefully in this chapter we will be able to give those who lead youth good counsel in both areas of concern.

The Church has published booklets on abuse that address children, youth, and spouses. The First Presidency and Twelve Apostles have stated:

"A great privilege of mortal life is bringing children into the world. In this process parents become co-creators with their Heavenly Father and are responsible to protect their children in every way. Children (and should we add youth and spouses) have a God-given right to that protection and to complete security and safety in the home. Parents should be willing to give their lives, if necessary, for the protection of their children" (*Child Abuse,* 1985). Note well this marvelous statement to which every member should subscribe. A man should, if necessary, give his life for his spouse, his little ones—even for his teenage children!

We also have abuse outside the home by other relatives, acquaintances, teachers, and occasionally even Church members called as advisers and leaders. I would hope we could say that children raised in Latter-day Saint homes were safe and secure. We ought to be able to do that. The Savior counseled that we should "become as little children" and that we "take heed that [we] despise not one of these little ones" (Matthew 18:3, 10).

In this same chapter of Matthew, the Lord reflects his fierce displeasure and terrible judgment for those who abuse children: "But whoso offend one of these little ones which believe in me, it were better for him that a millstone were hanged about his neck, and that he were drowned in the depth of the sea" (verse 6). Note that the footnote to this verse indicates that the Greek word translated as *offend* means to "cause to stumble." There are so many ways of offending our children, and abuse is the most destructive of all. Youth leaders would be wise not to assume that all under their direction are safe. We must be alert, watch carefully, and listen with our spirit. If you have an impression, share it with the bishop. He can discreetly question or observe until he knows. Of course, we do not want to suspect everyone, or teach the youth in a way that they assume no one can be trusted. Far and away the great hosts of parents, grandparents, family members, and leaders can be trusted. They have a right and an obligation to shower righteous love, hugs and kisses, caresses, and care on those close to them.

It is my belief that every child or youth will have a "special warning" when someone has ill or abusive motives in their touches and caresses. President Boyd K. Packer said, "No one has a right to touch you in places they should not" (*To Young Men Only* [Salt Lake City: The Church of Jesus Christ of Latter-day Saints]). There is a genuine warning which comes from the Spirit that youth should be taught to heed.

Satan also will pretend to warn them, but his influence will be distorted, telling children not to trust those who are true. He will put suspicions in their minds, suspicions that might be reinforced by some social workers or teachers who will not trust anyone. Sometimes these leaders themselves were abused, and they assume incorrectly that no one can be trusted. Satan will deliberately send out signals to destroy normal, healthy relationships, but there is always a way to detect him. "Satan can appear as an angel of light or can cause a burning in the bosom," taught Elder Mark E. Petersen. "But he can never bring peace."

Teach the youth that when things are normal and appropriate in their relationships with adults or others, they will have a sweet feeling of peace. Satan can never duplicate that feeling or bring a sweet peace. Our youth need to know that, because love, kindness, and proper hugs from parents and caring adults can be essential in building esteem and providing emotional and spiritual support.

Leaders and parents should be aware of those who are vulnerable. When I was 13 or 14, my parents divorced. I was attending junior high school. One day my teacher invited me out into the hall. The hall was about 100 yards long. We were all alone. The teacher walked up to me, unbuttoned my shirt, and began to rub my stomach. Spontaneously I did the right thing—I jumped back, quickly buttoned up my shirt, and said, "What are you doing?" He said, "I want to ask you some questions." Well, I wasn't a genie and he didn't need to rub my stomach to get answers! We returned to the classroom and that never happened again. I think, however, that he knew I was vulnerable because of my poor self-esteem, my parents' divorce, and our family being very poor. Two years later that teacher was arrested for molesting other young men, and he was sent to the Utah state penitentiary for two years.

Our son David was involved in Little League. One of the men who supervised the boys had a responsible position in the Church and was seemingly wonderful with young men. I had great respect for him. I supervised the league. One day David said to me, "Brother ——— is attracted to boys." I responded, "Dave, don't ever say that again. He is a good man and a fine leader." David was hurt and said, "Okay, if you don't want to know—but he is." That should have been enough of a signal to me, but I was young and naive, and I assumed that this leader's attention to the boys was motivated by the same spirit that mine was. This man also was later identified as a pedophile, or one with a perverted sexual attraction to children, and was sentenced to prison. On learning this, I was shocked; then I remembered my son's warning, which I had ignored. There will always be clues if we watch and listen for them.

We also need to clearly and directly teach our youth that homosexuality is a chosen behavior. President Marion G. Romney, in a meeting with the First Presidency and Presiding Bishopric years ago, said, "The God of Heaven will never put a female spirit in a male body or a male

70

spirit in a female body." Of course, he was not referring to the pitiful cases of nature's aberrations or deformities in which it is difficult to distinguish the sex of a child, but to those who are physically born male or female. This information is helpful to youth as they resolve their identity.

Some young men may appear effeminate, and some young women may appear more masculine. That is not an indication that they have been in some way biologically programmed to be other than what they truly are. They need healthy examples, and they need to be taught the doctrine of the Church with scriptural affirmation. There is so much foolishness and so many supposedly scientific studies that appear to vindicate those persons who choose homosexual behavior or take on a lesbian lifestyle. The answer to this whole question is given in the "The Family: A Proclamation to the World," by the First Presidency and the Quorum of the Twelve Apostles. This is the word of God: it answers the gender questions, emphasizes acceptable conduct, and teaches consequences for those who violate its tenets.

God bless this Church. It has resources to help all those who engage in perverted behavior. Along with booklets dealing with families, abuse, homosexuality, and addictions, we have well-trained Social Services resources, and particularly we have our priesthood leaders who have the mantle of God resting on them to bless the people.

Refer back to the chapters on justice and God's divine mercy for additional counsel on the need to use the Atonement to help heal the innocent as well as the guilty. Victims of incest, rape, other sexual violation, or indeed any forcible act on anyone can be totally healed. The God of heaven, who can create worlds without number, who can turn rivers upstream and remove mountains by the power of His word, can surely heal the innocent victims. Our Father in Heaven knows the past of the earthly parent and what he or she will do in the future. It must grieve Him when His little ones come to homes where they are not loved and cared for. But we can be confident that there will be compensating blessings for every moment of suffering, pain, distress, or hurt they experience. Even if these acts against them in their childhood or youth should turn them in the direction of transgression, we can be assured that a loving Father will be merciful, just, and kind.

Healing and removing such scars to us seems difficult, but not to

God. Jesus Christ through His Atonement can wash us clean and remove every fear, terror, indignity, pain, and sorrow. We may not always forget such things, but they can cease to bother us. Alma the younger is a good example. He talked of his past efforts to destroy the Church and other transgressions—or as he said, "iniquity"—but they ceased to bother him after his repentance.

Christ's Atonement can remove all pain and suffering from the innocent. He is available 24 hours a day, 365 days a year, as is our Father and God. When we turn the problem and pain over to them for their justice and mercy, miracles happen. The abused one, like Alma the younger, "will remember [the] pains no more," and a quiet sweetness and joy will fill his or her soul. All things are possible to God, but doing all things requires faith and forgiveness. The injured person must forgive the perpetrator and turn the matter completely over to Christ. Then, when this is done, the Atonement of the Lord Jesus Christ can be extended into every fiber of the abused innocent soul and thereby heal it completely.

Another challenge for parents and leaders of youth is to raise up a generation free from these terrible social illnesses. Use the doctrine, the proclamation on the family, the scriptures, and personal testimony to build a firm foundation in the lives of our youth. This problem is going to increase in the world, but it must not in the Church. There are thousands of voices that appeal to our youth. Your strong voice, early on, will give them the foundational teachings of the gospel that will set them on the right course for dating, marriage, and raising a family.

Now we have not addressed state and national laws as they relate to reporting abuse. In some states it is mandatory. However, the Church has a 24-hour-a-day hotline that leaders can call to receive counsel and direction, including clarification regarding local laws. Again, isn't this a wonderful Church that tends to so many needs in such a professional and compassionate way?

Some will be surprised to learn that many of the difficulties and concerns that we face today existed during the time of the Old Testament. Consider the following counsel from the book of Leviticus, chapters 18, 19, and 20:

"None . . . shall approach to any that is near of kin to him, to uncover their nakedness" (18:6).

Mothers and fathers should not be seen naked (18:7–8).

Other family members should not be seen naked, including sisters, nieces, and grandchildren (18:9–11). We have far too many grandchildren molested; this scripture implies that we must protect our grandchildren.

Do not commit adultery (18:20).

Do not commit acts of homosexuality (18:22).

Do not abuse the deaf and blind, verbally or otherwise (19:14).

Do not prostitute thy daughter (19:29).

Every one that curseth his father or his mother shall be surely put to death (20:9).

Adultery is a serious offense (20:10).

Of course, these three chapters carry far more detailed laws of the Old Testament. The interesting thing is how severe was the penalty, which apparently served as a significant deterrent.

We now live in the day of the broken heart and contrite spirit, which should come to us as we seek to repent. In most of the modern world, no one will be put to death or banished for these wrongs in our day, but the sin is as serious now as it was in ancient Israel.

Teach both young men and young women that those whom they date who are abusive—either physically or by demeaning them—will seldom change after marriage. The boyfriend who strikes his girlfriend will probably persist in this terrible conduct after marriage.

Years ago a good friend of mine brought his married son to see me. He had physically beaten up his wife and had done it many times before. It was so repulsive to me I was not certain I could counsel him properly. The fine-looking son in his mid-twenties wept as he told of what he had done to his wife. He swore to me that it would never happen again. His wife had left and taken the children. He said, "I have learned my lesson." We visited for an hour or so, and in my naiveté, I promised to talk to his wife and encourage her to come back. She was a good woman who loved the Church leaders and wanted to follow our counsel.

I learned that she had gone back to him, but when his anger returned he beat her up again and again. I did not know then what I understand now—that this type of behavior seldom changes in the abusive one. It requires counseling and a total trust in Christ. No one has a right to physically abuse anyone else. No one owns another. We all are

73

individuals. No one can force us—that is what the war in heaven was about.

A young woman whose boyfriend beats her should sever the relationship as soon as he touches her. If he threatens to harm her if she quits going with him, that is the time her father, brother, bishop, or other strong authority figure ought to step in to her defense. If necessary, involve the police. Young women who lose their temper and throw things that could cripple or maim a young man need the same counseling. Life demands discipline.

Preventative measures taken before marriage vows are made will save a great deal of mental and physical suffering.

Remind a young woman who feels it is unchristian to cut off a relationship because she thinks she should try to help her boyfriend that she does not have to be the one to administer counseling and support. Priesthood leaders and Social Services can do that. She should feel no guilt for breaking up with an abusive boyfriend.

Someone very close to us was going with a young returned missionary. They were ready to get married and were considering the date. The father had some uneasy feelings, as did the mother, but the daughter was certain she had found the young man to whom she wanted to be sealed. Then the parents began to get bits of feedback from the daughter. She apparently did things that irritated the young man. He scolded her when they went to dinner that she ate too much. Now this was a beautiful, well-proportioned young lady who was careful about her appearance. He criticized her shoes, her dresses, the classes she took. The romance seemed to turn from love to dominance, to power, to jealousy, and to constant demeaning. Thank goodness she was mature. She prayed, fasted, and returned his diamond ring. She is married now to someone who adores her. He loves everything about her. He has talked about her angelic beauty and character. He is far too gentlemanly ever to tear her down.

Remind our youth that a sealing in the temple is for all eternity, and that they need to choose someone who will be a friend, a lover, and a companion, one who will continue to be romantic into the eternities. Even a commitment to be married can and should be broken if personality and character flaws that could permanently damage the relationship are not discovered or acknowledged until after the engagement.

Teach youth that they need to fall in love with someone who loves the Lord more than themselves, someone who wants to be married in the right place at the right time by the right authority.

Britt McConkie, a brother of Elder Bruce R. McConkie, taught the following crucial principle: "When a young man or young woman marries someone who is either not a member of the Church or who is not worthy to go to the temple, *they have given up their agency.* They have turned it over to the less-active or nonmember husband or wife, and there will be no possibility of an eternal marriage and sealing blessing until and unless the companion decides he or she is ready. In this sense a marriage truly is damned (held back) until the nonmember or less-active companion changes his or her mind!"

The principle and concerns in this chapter are difficult to talk or write about. They just about break your heart. But one day all these evils will be done away with, perhaps later in the lives of our present-day youth! May God grant that prayer for the abused.

PART

3

LEADING IN PRACTICE

12

"The Strength of God Is in Us"

All of our lives, we have taught young men and young women to heed the Word of Wisdom. In the Old Testament, four young Hebrew men named Daniel, Hananiah, Mishael, and Azariah (who were later given the Babylonian names of Belteshazzar, Shadrach, Meshach, and Abed-nego) were chosen to receive training in King Nebuchad-nezzar's court. The king appointed them a daily provision of the king's meat and wine, with which he intended to nourish them for three years.

These four wonderfully wholesome young men, along with others who qualified, were selected because they were "well favoured, and skilful in all wisdom, and cunning in knowledge, and understanding science, and such as had ability in them to stand in the king's palace, and whom they might teach the learning and the tongue of the Chaldeans" (Daniel 1:4). The process of selection was interesting. Who knows how broadly they had to search for such healthy, well-balanced young men.

Despite their favored treatment, these four young men rejected the delicacies and wine of the king. Daniel "purposed in his heart that he would not defile himself with the portion of the king's meat, nor with the wine which he drank: therefore he requested of the prince of the eunuchs that he might not defile himself" (verse 8).

Although the individual entrusted to watch over Daniel and his friends feared to disobey the king, Daniel persuaded him to test them for 10 days against the others. At the end of the trial period these four lads were described thus: "Their countenances appeared fairer and fatter in flesh than all the children which did eat the portion of the king's meat" (verse 15). Then came the following significant blessing: "As for these four children, God gave them knowledge and skills in all learning and wisdom: and Daniel had understanding in all visions and dreams" (verse 17).

The final proof of God's promised blessings for obedience came when they stood before the king, and "he found them ten times better than all the magicians and astrologers that were in all his realm" (verse 20).

We have taught so often the blessings of the Word of Wisdom, and some wonder if it does any good. Let there be no doubt—the Word of Wisdom does indeed make a difference. Like Daniel, Shadrach, Meshach, and Abed-nego, we have equally sweet, wholesome youth who have lived the Word of Wisdom. Our minds and our physical bodies respond to proper nourishment. Our youth are not just in better physical condition—they also think more clearly. Someday we will understand better how all this works together—food, exercise, rest, and brain power—but for now it is enough to know that obedience to true principles brings untold blessings.

As members of the Church, we know that we should not use any substance that contains illegal drugs, has habit-forming ingredients, or is otherwise harmful. Some may choose to compromise this principle because certain caffeine drinks are not mentioned in the Word of Wisdom, or because we know that drinking them will not "keep us out of the temple," nor will it restrict our Church service. But we need not be commanded in all things. When we think of all the options, every variety of juice and wholesome drinks that add to our health ought to be considered first.

A great young missionary served in the Texas San Antonio Mission during the time I presided there. We have kept somewhat in touch over the years since. Steve Payne was a presiding zone leader and as fine a missionary as he could possibly be. He was totally committed to his call. He recently wrote me a letter and shared a personal experience. He is married to a lovely wife, has a beautiful family, and has earned a doctorate. He gave me permission to use his personal witness of the Word of

Wisdom. Entitled "Run and Not Be Weary," it is not unlike that of Daniel and his brethren:

"In 1975 I was attending Brigham Young University and was a member of the Air Force Reserve Officers Training Corp (AFROTC). I had joined the AFROTC in the hope of becoming a pilot, but in this waning year of the Vietnam War, the Air Force requirements for pilots had, well, plummeted (sorry about the bad play on words). As part of our training we were required to attend a six-week officers' boot camp during the summer break between semesters. My chances of getting one of the few pilot slots were slim to none unless I performed well at the summer encampment. Majoring in physics in college, I felt that the academics would most likely not be a significant challenge. However, there was one aspect of the camp that when I thought upon it left me with a chill of fear and apprehension. This was the daily one and one-half mile run. I had tried to run cross-country while in junior high school but found I didn't have the strength for it in my ankles. I would go in with my ankles taped often halfway up my calf just to keep them from twisting out from under me. Even with that, I would invariably end up last. On occasion I suffered the embarrassment of finishing with the knowledge that the officials had held up the following heat so that I wouldn't be mistaken as one of the varsity team finishes, I was so far behind the rest of my group. I hadn't done much running since that miserable junior high year.

"I traveled with four of my fellow BYU AFROTC cadets to our camp at Holoman Air Force Base in Alamagordo, New Mexico. As it turned out, we were the only LDS cadets in the Squadron of about 100. I ended up in a flight of about 25 by myself. There are very strict rules at boot camp, and one of them is 'lights out' at 10:00 P.M. The days were so full of training from before dawn to after dusk that we barely had time to get out of our day clothes for bed before lights out was called. The active duty officers would often patrol the barracks, randomly checking rooms. If anyone was caught out of bed it meant demerits and extra duties. I was therefore a little fearful of being caught at getting out of my bunk to kneel and say my prayers, not to mention what my roommate might think. I did it nonetheless and poured out my heart to my Father in Heaven. I acknowledged my physical weakness in running and pleaded with him to help me. In my prayer the promise of the Word of Wisdom

(Doctrine and Covenants 89:20) 'and shall run and not be weary, and shall walk and not faint' came to my mind. I told the Lord that I had lived the Word of Wisdom and that I *really* needed that blessing now in order for me to reach my goal.

"The next morning the squadron gathered on the parade ground and fell out by flight for the mile and a half run. When it came our flight's turn, I lined up with the rest at the starting line. I was still nervous but felt the Lord had heard my prayer. When the signal came, I ran out in the front of the pack only to find that after the first lap I had fallen back. The next lap I was in the middle, and by the end I was last in the flight. I was dumfounded and discouraged. Why hadn't the Lord answered my prayer? That night I went to the Lord in prayer a little frustrated, I'm sorry to say. I again pleaded my case as I had the night before. This time Psalm 40 came to my mind, and I realized that my Father in Heaven was providing me an opportunity to learn patience as well as faith.

"The next morning I approached the run with the same faith but a little more humbled from my previous night's heavenly admonishment. The results from that run were not different from the previous day: I was still last. I found, however, that by the end of the week I was not at the end, though still close to it. By the end of the second week I was finishing in the middle of the flight. I often found myself chanting to the cadence of my running, 'Run and not be weary. [Breath.] Walk and not faint. [Breath.] Run and not be weary . . . ' By the end of the third week I was near the front. From that point on I was running almost literally on the heels of the fastest man in our flight, if not the squadron. He ran cross-country for his college team. Although I couldn't beat him, neither could he lose me. I remember him taking glances back at me after trying to break away, only to find me right behind him.

"When we finished the final sprint to the end, something I had never been able to do before in my life, I saw that my 'running mate' was bent over and breathing heavily to recover. Although at first I felt just as spent, I found my strength and breath returning to me quickly. I then felt a prompting: 'Get back on the track and run alongside the guys that are having trouble in the back. Remember, you were there yourself not so very long ago. You know what it's like.' As I moved to the track I could sense the other finishers from our flight looking at me and, I'm sure, wondering, 'What does he think he's doing?' I ran up alongside the last man running in our flight and, after matching his pace, began encouraging him, 'You can do it; I know you can. When you succeed we all succeed. If you fail, we all fail. I'm with you all the way. *You can do it!*' And he did do it, and better than the day before.

"The next day after I finished and returned again to the track, to my surprise I was joined by my running mate. He chimed in with encouraging words, only now it was 'We know you can do it! *We're* with you all the way!' By the end of the week we had a group of early finishers surrounding the struggling runner, all motivating him on. When we got to the finish line, a cheer went up from the whole flight; he had made it just under the minimum required time. That night I again knelt in humble prayer, but now in thanks to a gracious Father in Heaven. He had not only fulfilled His promises of the Word of Wisdom to me personally, but He had also provided me the prompting of the Holy Ghost. Once I had been blessed, He had guided me to strengthen my struggling brother, and by so doing He brought increased unity within our flight of cadets. I had been blessed well above my original somewhat selfish request. Beyond the confirmation that the Lord keeps His promise, I had learned that along with a blessing, the Lord often includes a prompting to use that blessing to serve others that thereby all might be edified. I also learned how important it is to wait patiently on the Lord. I have ever since been grateful for those lessons."

Elder Hartman Rector has always had a wonderful spirit. When he was converted, it was a heart and soul conversion. He has been one of the greatest and most touching speakers in the Church. Many years ago I went to a zone conference with Elder Rector when he was a mission president. He had memorized the words of a great poem, which he shared with the missionaries. I immediately found the poem and memorized it also. It has been a strong influence in my life. I have seldom used it publicly, but I think I have said it several hundred times to myself:

"If"

If you can keep your head when all about you
Are losing theirs and blaming it on you.
If you can trust yourself when all men doubt you
Yet make allowance for their doubting too.

If you can wait without being tired by waiting
Or being lied to, don't deal in lies,
Or being hated, don't give way to hating,
And yet don't look too good or talk too wise.

If you can dream and not make dreams your master
If you think and not make thoughts your aim
If you can meet with triumph and disaster
And treat those two imposters just the same.
If you can bear to hear the truths you've spoken
Twisted by knaves to make a trap for fools.
Or see the things you gave your life to broken
And stoop and build them up again with worn out tools.

If you can make a heap of all your winnings
And risk it all on one turn at pitch and toss,
And lose and start again at the beginning
And never breathe a word about your loss.
If you can force your heart and nerve and sinew
To serve your aim long after they are gone
And then continue on when there is nothing in you
Except the will in them that says "keep on."

If you can talk with crowds and keep your virtue
Or walk with kings, nor lose the common touch;
If neither loving friend nor foe can hurt you
And have all men count with you, but none too much.
If you can fill the unforgiving minute
Of sixty seconds of full distance run,
Then yours is life and all that's in it
And, what is more, you'll be a man, my son.
(Rudyard Kipling.)

That poem is a pretty good measuring rod of how we are matching up to our potential. I will on occasion break the poem down line by line and see how I am personally measuring up.

It has been a blessing in my life to memorize great poetry, scripture, and sayings. I memorize those things that I always want to have with me. The wisdom of statements by the prophets and the counsel are definitely worth memorizing.

It has long been my belief that the body is always healing itself, or at least trying to. When I have occasionally had problems, I just think,

"Don't worry, your body is working to heal itself," and unless it is something that requires medical attention, the problem eventually goes away.

The strength of God is within us. It is in our bodies, which are temples of God, if we so live. And it is in our minds. Voltaire said, "No problem can stand the assault of sustained thinking." Parents and leaders, teach our youth the power of their own being, the miracle of who they are, and the wonderful things that can be wrought by them as they are faithful. Teach them to imagine the miracle of being co-creators with God in bringing children to earth, of being parents, building homes, having fulfilling employment and continuing to develop their minds and bodies. Youth will be fulfilled in life as they seek first the kingdom of God. Then will come into their lives the sweetness of all the gospel offers because of their righteousness. No matter how dark and evil the clouds are on the horizon, the dawning of the Millennial Christ will come.

13

"For We Wrestle Not against Flesh and Blood"

Many years ago when I was a much younger father, I was perusing an issue of the *Improvement Era* when I came across a poem that touched me deeply. The title was "Don't Send My Boy":

> Don't send my boy where your girl can't go
> and say there's no danger for boys you know,
> because they all have their wild oats to sow.
> There is no more excuse for my boy to be low
> than your girl; then please do not tell him so,
> this world's old lie is a boy's worst foe,
> To hell or the Kingdom they each must go.
>
> Don't send my boy where your girl can't go
> For a boy or girl, sin is sin you know,
> And my baby boy's hands are as clean and as white
> And his heart is as pure as your girl's tonight.
> That which would send the soul of your girl to the pits of hell
> Would send the soul of my boy there as well.

This new generation has monumental tests and trials over any previous generation of youth. A generation ago young women as a rule had a soft and modifying effect on young men. This is still true for most of our wonderful young women in the Church. Out in the world it is not always so. Many young women of both teen and college age are aggressive and foulmouthed, and they often act and behave in a most distasteful way.

A young mother with a son in elementary school called in to a talk television program and shared the disgusting phone calls her son had been receiving from his young female peers. The talk was vulgar, filthy, and essentially destructive. They criticized his soccer team, called him fat, and further abused him verbally. The mother was distraught and wanted to have the phone calls cease.

One day while driving, I watched as a university-aged young woman weaved in and out of traffic. She cut in front of a man, so he honked his horn. She flashed an obscene gesture and continued weaving through the traffic. I looked over at the man—he just shrugged his shoulders.

This generation is different. In fact, in some ways they have been legally required to change. For example, young people are forbidden to pray or refer to God or Christ in a positive way in any school setting. They cannot sing Christmas music, even though the holiday celebrates His birth. Yet on those same school grounds young people can profane the name of Christ and use the Lord's name in vain with multiple outbursts in a single sentence; they can curse a constant stream of ugliness that offends the soul; they can establish gay clubs and promote abortion, but they cannot pray or sing Christmas carols.

A man was on a national television talk show in Canada. He was a pedophile and was sharing his deeply perverted view with the public. He hoped pedophiles would come out into the open just as the homosexual community had done. He talked about "man-boy love" and his right to fulfill his sexual orientation. The program must have been watched by millions. I imagine there were great hosts of children—boys and girls—who listened to this pervert propound his beliefs. At the end of the program, someone asked if he were a Mormon. He responded that he was in good standing in the Church. When this was reported to me, I found out his full name and, on checking with our confidential records section, discovered that it was just as I had suspected. He had been a member of the Church but had been excommunicated for molesting young boys.

I contacted our public affairs director in Canada and gave her the information I had found out. She called the TV station and learned that the talk program had been canceled. There was no way to get back to that audience so we could vindicate the truth of our teachings and show this man for the evil liar he is.

The Boy Scouts of America organization has a videotape for training those who lead children. It is entitled *A Time to Tell*. It teaches adult leaders how to train and teach young men to be aware of those who may attempt to involve them in evil pursuits. Unquestionably it has helped many young men identify and successfully deal with such depraved individuals. Our youth need to be informed in an appropriate and delicate but very clear way.

We cannot ignore the problem or act as if such things were not happening. Satan has removed all subtlety. He is a master of lies and has influenced deeply the minds and opinions of powerful people both in and out of the media.

Our youth must be able to hear a clarion call and know that there are those who hold firm to integrity and honor. Of course, the best place in the world for this training to take place is in the home under the direction of a true patriarch and a blessed mother.

A few years ago only gay men who wanted to send a signal to other men of their orientation wore earrings. Now we see men wearing earrings in all walks of life, including professional athletes. Earrings are worn by movie stars, male models, businessmen, and construction workers.

Few Church members wear tattoos, and yet the outside world is making this practice more acceptable in society. Young people are wearing rings in their lips, tongues, cheeks, and eyebrows, and a string of them in their ears, and in their navels. Isaiah understood this foolishness. Consider his words as they relate to our day:

> The shew of their countenance doth witness against them; and they declare their sin as Sodom, they hide it not. Woe unto their soul! For they have rewarded evil unto themselves. . . .
>
> Moreover the Lord saith, Because the daughters of Zion are haughty, and walk with stretched forth necks and wanton eyes, walking and mincing as they go, and making a tinkling with their feet:
>
> Therefore the Lord will smite with a scab the crown of the head

of the daughters of Zion, and the Lord will discover their secret parts.

In that day the Lord will take away the bravery of their tinkling ornaments about their feet, and their cauls, and their round tires like the moon,

The chains, and the bracelets, and the mufflers,

The bonnets, and the ornaments of the legs, and the headbands, and the tablets, and the earrings,

The rings, and nose jewels,

The changeable suits of apparel, and the mantles, and the wimples, and the crisping pins,

The glasses, and the fine linen, and the hoods, and the vails.

And it shall come to pass, that instead of sweet smell there shall be stink; and instead of a girdle a rent; and instead of well set hair baldness; and instead of a stomacher a girding of sackcloth; and burning instead of beauty (Isaiah 3:9, 16–24).

President Boyd K. Packer has suggested that a "study of the doctrines of the gospel will improve behavior quicker than a study of behavior will improve behavior" (*Ensign,* Nov. 1986, p. 17). Our youth need to learn doctrine. The Lord will not leave rebelliousness unaddressed. In 1 Corinthians 3:16–17, the Apostle Paul declared: "Know ye not that ye are the temple of God and that the Spirit of God dwelleth in you? If any man defile the temple of God, him will God destroy; for the temple of God is holy, which temple ye are."

In the recent past I was visiting a stake in the East. The stake president told me of a bishop who had been released not long before. Immediately after his release, he began to wear a gold earring. He was in his forties. The adult ward members were a little exercised that a former bishop would wear an earring. Some of the young men in the ward started to question him about it because they knew they could not officiate in the sacrament service while wearing an earring. Well, this former bishop was offended, and pretty soon he stopped attending church. However, he came to the stake conference where I presided. When I greeted him he did not have the earring on, but I of course knew something of the background. I said, "I understand you are a little troubled over the attitude of some of the members about your wearing an earring." He gave me an earful of what had been said and told me how upset he was with the members' criticism. He concluded by saying, "I haven't been coming to church. It burns me up. I came to stake conference, but I'm not certain I am coming back to church."

I said, "Bishop, listen to me. Do you know what you are saying? You have been baptized into the only true and living Church. You have been sealed to your wife and children in the temple. You wear the garment; you have temple privileges; you hold the Melchizedek Priesthood. You served as a bishop, so you know the policy. I can't even comprehend that an earring means that much to you. The message you are sending to youth and adults alike is that earrings are more important than all the things precious and dear in the Church. What in the world are you thinking?"

It shocked him. He said, "Well, I didn't think about those things." I said, "Bishop, I don't want to do anything in my life that will test the faith of another member of the Church." Then I said, "You should get down on your knees and thank God for those who love you enough to warn you." I wondered how many young men and women would see *his* example and might choose *his* compromise as justification for them to compromise a far more serious commandment later on in their lives.

If we lead anyone away from the truth we will be held accountable. In Ephesians we read: "For we wrestle not against flesh and blood, but against principalities, against powers, against the rulers of the darkness of this world, against spiritual wickedness in high places" (Ephesians 6:12).

We need to be very sensitive with those of our youth who deviate and join the ways of the world, get tattoos, wear inappropriate hairstyles, dye their hair bright iridescent colors, and, for the young men, wear earrings. They need a course correction. However, the best way I know to correct them is that we *live in such a way that they respect us.* Then they become willing to sit down and reason together. And when you do sit down together, please use the scriptures to teach the doctrine. Be patient and always love them, and they generally will follow good inspired counsel.

You may say, "That doesn't sound like the way you handled that former bishop with the earring." True. I treated him as a former bishop, a high priest, and a temple recommend holder, in the spirit of Doctrine and Covenants 121:43: "Reproving betimes with sharpness, when moved upon by the Holy Ghost."

Remember, you can always tell when you reprove as "moved upon by the Holy Ghost." When you finish reproving you still have the Spirit with you. If someone asked for a blessing, you could turn right around and do it.

In Sydney, Australia, where I now reside, the annual gay and lesbian Mardi Gras was held recently. It lasted for several days. The highlight of the event was a parade which over 700,000 people attended, some of whom had come from overseas just to see it. Many people brought their children, and many came as families. Judging from the reports I read and heard, it would have been better for children to gaze into an open cesspool! You only have to imagine the lewdness, the evil, the perverse dress and costuming. I am convinced that the pen of man cannot describe the revulsion good men and women must feel in such situations. Can you imagine that any caring parent could take a child to such an activity? The images seen there will remain with the children throughout their lives! Think about beautiful, innocent, wonderful children being exposed to a modern-day Sodom. We should know better. We should do better.

Don't send my boy where your girl can't go, and don't send my boy where your girl should not go.

Satan seduces the children of men with an image of the exciting, pleasurable, fun things of the world. He is ever deceitfully hiding the consequences. Solomon described the subtle temptation to which our youth are exposed:

> At the window of my house I looked through my casement,
> And beheld among the simple ones, I discerned among the youths, a young man void of understanding,
> Passing through the street near her corner; and he went the way to her house,
> In the twilight, in the evening, in the black and dark night:
> And, behold, there met him a woman with the attire of an harlot, and subtil of heart.
> (She is loud and stubborn; her feet abide not in her house:
> Now is she without, now in the streets, and lieth in wait at every corner.)
> So she caught him, and kissed him, and with an impudent face said unto him,
> I have peace offerings with me; this day have I payed my vows.

Therefore came I forth to meet thee, diligently to seek thy face, and I have found thee.

I have decked my bed with coverings of tapestry, with carved works, with fine linen of Egypt.

I have perfumed my bed with myrrh, aloes, and cinnamon.

Come, let us take of our fill of love until the morning: let us solace ourselves with loves.

For the goodman is not at home, he is gone a long journey:

He hath taken a bag of money with him, and will come home at the day appointed.

With her much fair speech she caused him to yield, with the flattering of her lips she forced him.

He goeth after her straightway, as an ox goeth to the slaughter, or as a fool to the correction of the stocks;

Till a dart strike through his liver; as a bird hasteth to the snare, and knoweth not that it is for his life.

Hearken unto me now therefore, O ye children, and attend to the words of my mouth.

Let not thine heart decline to her ways, go not astray in her paths.

For she hath cast down many wounded: yea, many strong men have been slain by her (Proverbs 7:6–26).

How often Satan mocks and laughs at the foolish ones he has ensnared and led to hell. Please, when you share the above passage with young men, remind them clearly of the consequences of giving in to temptation.

Yes, let us protect our youth against the tide of the day. We cannot, we must not, give way. We must fight with every ounce of energy we have.

President Joseph F. Smith said: "After we have done all we can for the course of truth and withstood the evils men have brought upon us, and been overwhelmed by their wrongs, it is still our duty to stand. We must not give up, we cannot lie down. Great causes are not won in a single generation. To stand firm in the face of overwhelming opposition, and to continue on is the courage of faith. And the courage of faith is the courage of progress. Men who have this divine quality cannot stand still. They are not creatures of their own wisdom or power; they are instrumentalities of a higher or divine purpose" (*Gospel Doctrine,* 5th ed. [Salt Lake City: Deseret Book Co., 1939], p. 119).

Great causes are not won in a single generation. Ours is a duty to stand firm so that our youth can see models of those who are rock solid, steadfast, and true.

14

The Sins of Babylon

In the South, a beautiful 18-year-old girl was voted homecoming queen. She was popular, respected, and, most important of all, she was a true Latter-day Saint. Some said she was the most beautiful and popular girl in high school. She loved the youth of her ward—the talented and the less talented. She was a hundred percenter in all of her church activities—seminary, Young Women, sacrament meeting, and her own private religious habits.

On the night she graduated from high school, she was with some LDS friends in the home of the stake president after the graduation exercises. There were, as I recall, about eight or nine LDS students in the entire school. They were going to the graduation dance together. She told her friends, "I have to go on an errand, but I should be back by 9:00 P.M. If I am not here by then, go to the dance without me." By the agreed-upon time, she had not returned, so the rest of the group went on to the dance. About ten minutes later she returned to find everyone gone. The stake president's wife advised, "Go on to the dance. You will have to go in alone, but I'm sure you will quickly find our group of LDS students."

However, she didn't feel she could go to the dance alone. She could not be persuaded to change her mind. She then said, "I think I will pick up a girlfriend and go to a movie. I don't want to go home this early on graduation night." She called her friend, then left to pick her up. On the way to the movie the girls decided to drop into a convenience store to get some candy and treats. A man about 20 years old was the clerk on duty that night. He was a member of the Church, but he was faithless. He seldom missed a meeting, because he loved the sociality, but he didn't pray or read the scriptures and apparently had little interest in the gospel. No doubt he did read the pornographic magazines that the store sold!

When he saw this special young woman, he asked her for a date when he got off work that night. She said, "I'm sorry but I have a date. My girlfriend and I are going to a movie." "What about tomorrow night?" he asked. She responded, "I'm busy." He pressed, "What about Sunday night?" She then said, "Please, I am trying to be kind, but I don't want to go out with you." The girls then went to the movie and returned home about midnight.

The young woman's 19-year-old brother was still up when she arrived. He had just received his mission call. They sat in the living room and talked together until about 2:30 A.M. Finally she said, "I'm tired; I'm going to bed." Her brother replied, "I'm hungry; I'm going to the kitchen for a dish of cereal." He fixed himself the cereal, returned to the living room, and turned on the TV. His sister went upstairs to her bedroom. As she started to undress for bed, someone stepped out of the shadows. It was the young man from the convenience store, and he had a switchblade in his hand. The young woman's mother overheard her daughter say, *"Please don't! That is the most precious thing I have in my life. I have never given it to anyone else, and I can't give it to you."* Her mother thought her daughter was having a bad dream. She shook her husband and said, *"You had better go to your daughter—she must be having a nightmare."* Her dad swung his feet off the bed just as they heard a terrific scream!

The young man had lunged at the young woman, and she had caught the knife blade in her hand. When he pulled it back it cut her fingers to the bone. Then he stabbed her above the breast and severed the main arteries to the heart. Quick as a flash, he ran out of her door. As her father raced to his daughter, he saw the shadow of a man running down the steps. When he reached her room, she took only a few steps toward him before falling into his arms, where she died almost instantly.

The brother had heard the scream and was just in time to see some-one run out of the door. He chased him and caught up with him about a block away. The knife-wielding young man turned around and struck him. The blade went through his forearm. The attacker then pulled the knife out and lunged at him again. He recognized the young man and held both arms up in a defenseless position. Then the young man ran off and back to his home.

I met this young woman's brother at an Aaronic Priesthood encamp-ment a few days before he was to report for his mission. He told me what I have just shared with you. His arm was still bandaged when I talked with him. He said that his sister had loved everyone and every-one loved her. She had helped activate young women who had not been attending Church meetings and activities. She had, through her exam-ple, even helped convert individuals to the Church.

This lovely young woman lived only a short life, but she lived it vir-tuously and beautifully. She didn't have much time to fill her mission on earth. I was told there were more than 2,000 people at her funeral! Even in her death she was a great missionary. I have told her story to youth all over the Church. Her name has been carried across the world, and she has done a tremendous amount of missionary work through my sharing this story, which is as accurate as I can recall.

A young man of about fifteen years of age was involved in drugs. He went to Las Vegas, where he needed money to support his addiction. He went to a convenience store, where he held up the clerk, a married woman with three or four children, and demanded money. While this woman was pulling the money out of the cash register to give to him, she reportedly asked, "Why are you doing this?" He then raised the pis-tol to her forehead and pulled the trigger! One moment a sweet mother—happy, conscientious, helping to support the family—was standing at the counter, and a minute later she was lying on the floor, dead.

The police caught the young man a few blocks away. They put him in jail and notified his family. About six weeks later his home ward bishop was able to arrange his schedule to go to Las Vegas to meet with this young man. The officers had apparently cut his hair and put him in clean prison clothes; while in jail, he had not been abusing drugs. During the interview, the bishop said, "We desperately need to know what we could have done to keep you from being in this situation. Surely as bishop, I or your advisers, your parents—all of us could have helped if we had known what to do." The youth said, "You couldn't have done anything." The bishop acknowledged to this young man, "I realize it is too late to help you, but please let us know what to do to keep someone else from ever being in jail for murder." Again came the same response, "You couldn't have done anything. I was rebellious and I chose to be rebellious."

The bishop then asked him if he knew when he had started rebelling, and he answered that it was when he was about eleven years old. "What happened at eleven years of age to cause you to rebel?" he asked the young man. "I began to listen to hard rock music, then metal rock, then acid rock, and finally death rock," was the reply.

Our youth need to understand that they ought not to confront other youth or anyone else when faced with a potentially dangerous situation. You can never be sure whether they are on drugs or in Satan's grip so much that even taking another life is done without hesitation or conscience.

One day I was following a station wagon down State Street in Salt Lake City when it began to go slower and slower. I assumed the driver was trying to be funny. There were half a dozen teenagers in the wagon. I moved over into another lane to pass, and they pulled into that lane in front of me. I switched back, and so did they. By now they were going really slowly, and I could hear them laughing. I honked the horn and motioned for them to move over. One of the young men in the back seat leaned down, pulled out a rifle, and aimed it at me. I held up my hands and backed off. The gun may not have been loaded, and they may have been just smarting off, but maybe they weren't! It was not worth taking the risk.

Some youth today feel power when they carry knives or other weapons. It is best just to give up your wallet without an argument if someone attempts to rob you. You cannot win, or even quarrel, when you encounter someone on drugs. Of drug abusers we sometimes hear that "their brains are fried"—this is probably a pretty accurate description.

We do live in a modern Babylon. However, we can walk through it, in part by following the Master's counsel in the Sermon on the Mount:

"Whosoever shall smite thee on thy right cheek, turn to him the other also. And if any man will sue thee at the law, and take away thy coat, let him have thy cloak also. And whosever shall compel thee to go a mile, go with him twain" (Matthew 5:39–41).

The Savior counseled wisely for our day: "Agree with thine adversary quickly, whiles thou art in the way with him" (Matthew 5:25). At first that seems to be strange counsel coming from the Lord, and yet it fits perfectly with what I have described above. It is far better to surrender a wallet, lose an argument, or avoid a confrontation than to lose your life or have your family threatened. Again, we do not know the depth of evil of our adversary, or even whether he is on drugs. There is a wonderful protection and peace that comes from following the Lord's direction.

"Road rage" is an accurate description of a recent phenomenon on our country's highways. I heard of a woman who was on her way home and unintentionally offended another driver. He swore at her and followed her home. He and his friend and both of their wives were in the car. The woman ran into her house and locked the door. They broke into her home and beat her up. After the men beat her severely, knocking out one tooth and breaking another, their wives picked up a plastic vacuum hose and continued to beat the woman!

Teach the young men and young women that the tendency to fight back, even if they are right, is sometimes not a good solution. There is a comforting verse in 1 Nephi: "The time soon cometh that the fulness of the wrath of God shall be poured out upon all the children of men; for he will not suffer that the wicked shall destroy the righteous. Wherefore, he will preserve the righteous by his power" (1 Nephi 22:16–17).

Some of our youth walk dangerously close to Babylon. They feed on the fringe, feeling safe, but there is no safety in sinning whether a little or a lot. As we consider the trend in our days, we gain great insight from the Book of Mormon. Mormon was a great and wonderful prophet. His counsel to his son Moroni is with loving charity and in the tender kindness of a parent. In his account Mormon teaches this profound truth for our day: "The judgments of God will overtake the wicked; and it is by the wicked that the wicked are punished" (Mormon 4:5).

Think now, who is it that kills gang members and hoodlums? Other gang members and hoodlums. What destroys the adulterer, the homosexual, the prostitute? The disease that the wicked pass on to the wicked! (The last volume I wrote to youth leaders did not mention AIDS because health scientists had not identified it at the time. Now even children know about AIDS.)

Remember, "it is by the wicked that the wicked are punished." Think of needles, drugs, and rebellious youth giving each other drugs. Who in my generation would ever have supposed that high schools would be campaigning for gay clubs and that singing Christmas carols would be banned? What an utterly ridiculous world we now live in.

We must live in the world, but we should not be of the world. This is marvelous counsel. We cannot feed around the edges of Babylon without being enticed closer and closer to evil.

President David O. McKay taught: "No act is ever committed without first having been justified in the mind." Before our youth sin, they will always have a strong warning. President Packer taught priesthood leaders that they will never make a serious mistake without a strong warning. When priesthood leaders attend to the Lord's business, they are entitled to His Spirit. When decisions are made or actions performed that are contrary to the will of the Lord, the bishop or stake president will be warned. They can override the warning, but sometime they will find that they have made a serious, generally embarrassing mistake. We cannot go back and undo some things, try as we may. Often all we can do is simply make a decision that we will not override the warning again and then keep that commitment. Parents and advisers, teach our youth this principle.

This is a chapter I did not want to write, but it is required by the world in which we live. Someone said, "If you don't go near a cliff, you will not fall over the edge." If you keep both feet firmly planted in Zion, you will feel no attraction to Babylon.

Hopefully we can say, "Master our youth are secure and safe, gathered into the garners, against the winds where the storm cannot penetrate against them."

15

Seminary—a Godsend

Elder Neal A. Maxwell has said, "I'm not sure our young people can survive spiritually today without seminary." Possibly that is all that needs to be said in this chapter, but let me include some additional thoughts for consideration.

I agree with Elder Maxwell with all my heart and soul. In the short twenty-five years since my first book, *A Generation of Excellence,* was published, conditions have changed so dramatically that this book of necessity covers issues that were only casually mentioned in my earlier writings to and about youth. In fact, morals, character, integrity, work ethic, heroes, and similar ideals have spiraled downward to an all-time low—and for certain have not yet bottomed out. We had better become involved as never before with our youth.

The one great, overruling confidence I have is that this Church is led by apostles and prophets of God. We have been counseled, taught, and trained as youth leaders. We have every tool we need to bring our youth safely through.

In general conference in April 1983, President Boyd K. Packer gave us inspired counsel that has increased in importance each succeeding year. The problems were serious for our youth in 1983, and thus came the warning voice of an apostle and prophet of God: "Without guidance, your student may choose another elective instead of seminary, or another course instead of an institute class. That would surely be a mistake. It would be like adding one more brick to the house of knowledge when there is little mortar to hold it all together. Parents, encourage, even insist, that your students register for seminary or institute. Presidents, bishops, youth leaders, you are responsible to encourage every youngster, without exception, to enroll. Few things you do will benefit them quite as much.

"Students, if your values are in place, you will not hesitate to forego an elective class that may decorate your life in favor of instruction which can hold together the very foundation of it. Then, once enrolled, attend, study, and learn. Persuade your friends to do the same. You will never regret it; this I promise you" (*Ensign,* May 1983, p. 67).

Then, in the same spirit of Elder Maxwell's statement, Elder Packer reminded us of the "prophetic preparation" needed for our youth: "In the history of the Church there is no better illustration of the prophetic preparation of this people than the beginnings of the seminary and institute program. These programs were started when they were nice, but were not critically needed. They were granted a season to flourish and to grow into a bulwark for the Church. They now become a godsend for the salvation of modern Israel in a most challenging hour. We are now encircled. These are the last days, foreseen by prophets in ancient times" (Boyd K. Packer, *Teach the Scriptures* [Salt Lake City: Church Educational System, 1978]).

It would seem that if we understood the warning voice and the spirit of Elder Maxwell's and Elder Packer's statements, we would move forward with tremendous energy to see that every potential student is enrolled in seminary. Bishops may take one or more ward council meetings and discuss the need for youth to enroll in seminary. Then the council should use their collective knowledge and experience to formulate a plan to implement the most thorough seminary enrollment ever launched in the ward. There is a leadership principle that states, "Use all the tools in your toolbox." That is what every ward and branch must do.

President Ezra Taft Benson gave wonderful, strong counsel regarding our college students and their participation in the institute program. The same counsel could be given to seminary-age youth. Just replace the word *institute* with *seminary,* and the statements will carry: "As a watchman on the tower, I feel to warn you that one of the chief means of misleading our youth and destroying the family unit is our educational institutions. There is more than one reason why the Church is advising our youth to attend colleges close to their homes where institutes of religion are available. It gives the parents the opportunity to stay close to their children, and if they become alerted and informed, these parents can help expose some of the deceptions of men. . . .

"Today there are much worse things that can happen to a child than not getting a full education. In fact, some of the worse things have happened to our children while attending colleges led by administrators who wink at subversion and amorality. Said Karl G. Maeser, 'I would rather have my child exposed to smallpox, typhus fever, cholera, or other malignant and deadly diseases, than to the degrading influence of a corrupt teacher. It is definitely better to take chances with an ignorant but pure-minded teacher than with the greatest philosopher who is impure'" (Conference Report, Oct. 1970, p. 22).

And before President Benson, President Kimball warned us. You will note the great concern he has for the youth: "You are all aware and we need not impress you further, because of your work in the wards and stakes, that these are days of great difficulties among the youth, particularly those between the ages of 12 and 21. Already we can see the hand of the Lord beginning to work. You will help to bring the focus of the time to young men of these critical ages; and when we refer to the young men, we mean the girls also. So all through your ministry remember, nothing should be secondary to placing great emphasis on the work of the Aaronic Priesthood. We urge you to work as a team in leading the Aaronic Priesthood, to work with the auxiliaries to see to it that they function in an auxiliary capacity, but always with the thought in mind of magnifying the priesthood and of making certain that no auxiliary takes ascendancy over the priesthood. This must always be in your minds as you plan your work."

In his loving, special way, President Kimball pleaded: "Secular knowledge, important as it may be, can never save a soul nor open the celestial kingdom nor create a world nor make a man a god, but it can be most helpful to that man who, placing first things first, has found the way to eternal life and who can now bring into play all knowledge to be his tool and servant. . . .

"Youth, beloved youth, can you see why we must let spiritual training take first place? Why we must pray with faith, and perfect our own lives like the Savior's? Can you see that the spiritual knowledge may be complemented with the secular in this life and on for eternities, but that the secular without the foundation of the spiritual is but like the foam upon the milk, the fleeting shadow?

"Do not be deceived! One need not choose between the two but only as to the sequence, for there is opportunity for one to get both simultaneously; but can you see that the seminary courses should be given even preferential attention over the high school subject; the institute over the college course; the study of the scriptures ahead of the study of the man-written texts; the association with the Church more important than clubs, fraternities, and sororities; the payment of tithing more important than paying tuition and fees?

"Can you see the ordinances of the temple are more important than the Ph.D. or any and all other academic degrees?" (Spencer W. Kimball, *Life's Directions* [Salt Lake City: Deseret Book Co., 1962], p. 173).

Consider doing all of these things, and more:

1. Write a sweet letter to each potential seminary student inviting him or her to enlist in this vital program. Begin each individually addressed letter personally to each student. All the letters can have the same information, but each one should be personalized to the individual from the bishopric, with the earnest, strong, feeling that the bishopric has for seminary. All the students will read the letter, and most will be impressed.

2. Enlist the Young Men and the Young Women advisers to make personal visits.

3. Use quorum and class presidencies as peer influences to visit and talk to those not committed to enroll in seminary.

4. Have home teachers counsel with parents (sometimes parents resist having to transport students to early morning seminary). They need to be told that the little time this demands will be only a fraction of the time they will put in to rescue their youth if they falter along the way. This is preventative maintenance. Also, some parents need doctrinal convincing and counsel from the bishop.

5. Use the closest friends of those not inclined to enroll to help persuade them.

In other words, we need to make a list of every young person of seminary age who is not enrolled in seminary; then we need to provide a spiritual and friendly assault that will persuade even those most resistant. We can do that. Three holy prophets of God have warned us. For our generation of excellence, the counsel has never been more relevant.

President Hinckley seems to mention seminary every time he speaks to youth. He has repeatedly counseled youth on its value. It would be interesting to see the totality of emphasis put forth regarding seminary by the First Presidency and Twelve over the past few years. I am confident we would be amazed. This issue of enrolling youth into seminary should be a top priority.

Those we cannot persuade to enroll at the commencement of the school year should be invited to enroll at the end of the semester or break. The same great effort should be made, for conditions may have changed to bring about a positive response.

President Boyd K. Packer in one of our training meetings stated, "We cannot comprehend the moment of history that we are experiencing." We can see this also but not nearly so clearly as those who are seers. We can, however, find the wisdom to follow their counsel.

I have a firm belief that seminary teachers receive a great deal of inspiration when they teach. From experience I know that much of this inspiration is designed by the Lord for specific individuals. I was very much aware of this when I taught seminary. On one occasion I had a lesson prepared for the next morning, a lesson that followed our instruction and the outline. That day I awoke at a very early hour. I lay there and thought about the lesson. I had a strong impression that one of the students was going through a stiff spiritual test. I got up and prepared a lesson from the impressions I was receiving. That morning at seminary, I said, "I awakened early this morning. One of you needs this lesson today." I then began to teach the lesson I had prepared early that morning. One young man began to weep. He wept through most of the lesson. When class was over he waited around until everyone had left. Then he humbly said, "I guess you know who the lesson was for." I responded that I did, and then he told me of the wrestle he had had with evil spirits at the same time I had gotten up to prepare the lesson.

This happened many times for different students' needs over the time I taught seminary. Seminary teachers are so important, and during such a critical period of time they are needed as never before. They need to be examples to our youth, having good marriages, temple sealings, a deep and abiding testimony, and, for the brethren, the Melchizedek Priesthood. All youth will be founded in the doctrine of the Church if they will faithfully attend. They will understand and know the scriptures and their application to life. They will have their testimonies reinforced and their religion personalized.

Oh, what a blessing seminary teachers are in this wonderful church! Teachers must be called and selected with great care. In my book *A Generation of Excellence,* I described what I call "the impact teacher." Today, as never before, we need such impact teachers. And the greatest impact a teacher should have is on spirituality. I heard Elder Bruce McConkie state at a Grace Idaho Stake conference, "No other talent exceeds spirituality."

Imagine the influence and impact on the life of a young man or woman when we lift them spiritually. They experience a growing self-esteem and confidence, they receive answers to life's hard questions, their range of difficult choices narrows, and they become endowed with a powerful, sweet, inner strength.

We must influence our youth to set proper values. A teacher modeling high moral values has a tremendous influence on seminary students and how they will handle stress, discipline, relationships with other people, respect for spouse, home influence, and the like. Therefore, a teacher's home life must be only of the highest quality. It will be difficult for seminary students to have much confidence in a teacher if the teacher's children wear inappropriate earrings (male and female); have tattoos, wild hair styles, or dyed hair; dress in a rebellious or worldly fashion (extreme); do not attend church or go on a mission; date nonmembers; or exhibit other immoral behavior.

Years ago I was in the Illigan Stake in the Philippines. We were reorganizing the stake leadership. A righteous sister who had served as a counselor in the district and then the stake Relief Society presidency was to be released. She didn't want to be released. I interviewed her finally and declared, "We have prayed about it; we feel at peace with the Spirit; it is the right thing to do." She said, "I do not agree. I will not accept a release. I want to continue on in my calling." Finally I responded, "Well, the decision has been made. We will release you this morning." She was a very unhappy and outspoken woman.

After the business of the stake, the music, and a few speakers, I felt prompted to call on this woman to speak. It was risky—against my better judgment—but I felt impressed. When she came to the stand, she told of our interview and how she had acted. She said that she resented the action of being released and did not feel good about it. Then, with deep emotion, she said, "I prayed while I was waiting for conference to start. I opened my scriptures to Doctrine and Covenants 64 and started reading verses 35–36: 'And the rebellious shall be cut off out of the land of Zion, and shall be sent away, and shall not inherit the land. For, verily I say that the rebellious are not of the blood of Ephraim, wherefore they shall be plucked out.'"

After she had read this she said, "The rebellious are not of the blood of Ephraim, and I am of the blood of Ephraim. I do not want to lose that blessing." Then she added, "I will do anything the Lord asks me to do, and I accept my release."

Our youth need to understand this same scripture: "The rebellious are not of the blood of Ephraim." As we discussed in another chapter, obedience is a wonderful privilege that wisdom and understanding would dictate we follow. What a marvelous freedom and what tremendous doors are open to those who are obedient. However, it is going to take the combined effort of parents, quorums, classes, advisers, bishoprics, and heavenly sentinels to bring our youth through.

Seminary is a godsend. It is an inspired, timely program that will yet prove more important than we would ever suppose.

16

"And the Day Shall Come That the Earth Shall Rest"

Several years ago I was in a general Young Men board meeting. At the close of the meeting we invited one of our general board members, Terry Nofinger, to give a spiritual thought. He told of being a 13-year-old Scout on a winter camp at Tracy Wigwam in the mountains east of Salt Lake City. Several feet of snow were on the ground. This particular night the whole troop was in the cabin. He recounted: "My Scoutmaster came to me and said, 'Terry, let's go for a walk.' We put on our heavy coats and went out into the clear, cold night. There was a full moon. The pines were laden with snow, and we walked on top of the snow, which had frozen solid enough to do that. When we were about 50 yards from the cabin, my Scoutmaster said, 'Terry, would you feel all right if we knelt here and have a prayer?' I agreed. We knelt and my Scoutmaster offered a prayer. When he finished he said, 'Terry, do you pray?' I said that I didn't. The Scoutmaster then said, 'Don't you think it is a good idea?' I thought for a moment and then said, 'Yes, I think it is a good idea.' The Scoutmaster then said, 'Terry, will you pray every morning and night for the rest of your life?'"

Terry said he never would make a commitment unless he intended to keep it. Even as a young man he had this quality. He thought for a long moment and determined that praying was a good idea and he ought to do it. He continued: "I promised my Scoutmaster that night, after kneeling in the deep snow under a full moon, that I would pray morning and night the rest of my life." Then he turned to the Young Men General Presidency and said, "I want my Scoutmaster Vaughn Featherstone to know that I have prayed every morning and night since that experience."

I have often wondered how important the setting was—beautiful white snow, a full moon, kneeling under great pines laden with snow. There is something about nature that often brings out the very best in us.

When I was a young Scout, our Scoutmaster, Bruford Reynolds, took us to that same Tracy Wigwam Camp. I remember to this day a sign on the cabin door: "A Scout does not wantonly destroy property." As a young man I knew that included the trees and nature's beauty in the canyons. We were trained when we went camping to return everything to its natural state so that no one could tell anyone had camped there overnight. Now the Scouting organization calls this "no-trace camping."

Another time when I was Scoutmaster, we went to Camp Steiner. We took some of the older young men and hiked in to the Four Lakes Basin. As you can well imagine, it was only a short time before the troop began to stretch out. The older, stronger boys were setting a pretty good pace. The younger boys were sagging a little behind. I was in about the middle of the pack. I had memorized the Sermon on the Mount and began to quote it as we hiked down the trail. The boys out front began to slow down, and the boys at the rear picked up the pace. Soon we were walking down this beautiful trail in the high Uintas in a large cluster.

Through the years I have always known that it was the great spiritual, natural, clean, wholesome setting of a high mountain trail, beautiful lakes, meadows, and pines that gave me the perfect setting to share the Sermon on the Mount with the Scouts. I could have shared it in a classroom at the ward meetinghouse, and it would have been okay, and they might have listened some, but being out in those magnificent Uintas brought a special teaching moment.

Grady Bogue, a university professor in Louisiana, gave a great talk in which he quoted these beautiful lines from Elspeth Huxley's 1959 novel *The Flame Trees of Thika:* "'The best way to find things out is not to ask questions at all. If you fire off a question it is like firing off a gun—bang it goes and everything takes flight and runs for shelter; but if you sit quite still and pretend not to be looking, all the little facts will come and peck around your feet, situations will venture forth from thickets, and intentions will creep out and sun themselves on a stone; and if you are very patient, you will see and understand a great deal more than the man with a gun does'" (in *Vital Speeches,* Jan. 1, 1997).

It seems easy to identify those who love the out-of-doors and the grand designs in nature. They seem to draw a special strength and character from the soil, the wondrous creations of God, the wild birds and animals. This is a glorious earth upon which we live. I believe a special kind of healing takes place when we spend time in the lofty mountains with sparkling rivers and streams, watching eagles and other mighty birds. Who does not stand in awe of a great Monarch Pine or wonder at the incredible beauty of an emerald-colored lake resting among the pines. Over the years I have watched boys turn into men during a one-week campout in the high wilderness.

George Dawson was a great Canadian engineer and explorer. He was small in stature and had serious respiratory diseases that took his life in his early fifties. He worked summer and winter surveying, exploring, and doing engineering work in the vast, northern wilderness of Canada. The northern city of Dawson Creek is named for him.

After he died he was eulogized with this wonderful tribute:

> And tell him the men he worked with
> Say, judging as best they can;
> That in lands that try manhood hardest
> He was tested and proven a man!

The ways of nature are not always easy, but we learn valuable lessons and gain something every time we experience them.

In the Midwest is a Boy Scouts of America council called the Dan Beard Council. Another great Scouter, Hamlin Garland, paid the following tribute to Dan Beard:

> Do you fear the force of the wind,
> The slash of the rain, go face them
> And fight them, be savage again.

Go hungry and cold like the wolf.
Go wade like the crane.
The palms of your hand will toughen,
The skin on your forehead will tan,
You'll be rugged and swarthy and weary;
But you'll walk like a man.

What a blessing the great out-of-doors is. The Boy Scouts of America has a large Scout ranch called Philmont. It is located just outside of Cimmaron, New Mexico, in the northeast area of the state. I believe with recent acquisitions that it is approximately 139,000 acres of land. Each year about 18,000 Scouts and Venturers (formerly Explorers) visit the ranch to take high-adventure backpacking treks into the Rocky Mountains. They are exposed to nature and taught all about the wildlife, both flora and fauna. As they sit around a campfire and look at the stars, all nature seems to come alive for them.

As a boy working on my Eagle Scout rank, the most exciting merit badges and yet the most difficult for me were those for bird study, camping, pioneering, and lifesaving. However, they were those I learned most from. Now the Scouting program has expanded to include nature and other earth and environmental science merit badges. Our Scouts of today are being trained to respect and care for our planet.

The Lord said, "I, the Lord, stretched out the heavens, and built the earth, my very handiwork; and all things therein are mine" (D&C 104:14). And my, oh my—what a handiwork it is! A great Scoutmaster helped me to appreciate nature and the out-of-doors. I have taught and modeled what I learned from him.

John Gardner states in his book *Self-Renewal:* "Young people do not assimilate values of their group by learning words (*truth, justice,* etc.) and their definitions. They learn attitudes, habits, and ways of judging. They learn these in intensely personal transactions with their immediate family or associates. They learn them in the routines and crises of living, but they also learn them through songs, stories, drama, and games. They do not learn ethical principles; they emulate ethical or unethical people. They do not analyze or list the attributes they wish to develop; they identify with people who seem to them to have these attributes. That is why young people need models, both in their imaginative life and in their environment, models of what man at his best can be."

110

I learned from Bruford Reynolds in intensely personal transactions with a few boys and a great leader. I learned to emulate an ethical, nature-loving leader. I could identify him with "what a man at his best can be."

For 56 years, since I was a Scout and was taught to care for nature, I have not thrown papers, cans, or garbage from the car as we traveled. Our sons always carry out the trash when they float the river. In fact, our family loves to float the white-water rivers, and we carry everything out. We practice to this day "no-trace camping." We don't kill the birds or cut down or carve in the trees.

Scouting is a worldwide organization. The Boy Scouts of America has more than five million registered men and boys. In the Scout Oath, each Scout repeats the promise to do his duty to God and his country. All countries showcase some part of God's handiwork. A man who reverences God and country will be a model for boys, as Bruford Reynolds was to me. A reverence for God is a reverence for all his creations.

A couple of years ago our family, including some 20 or so of our grandchildren, floated the main Salmon River. One early morning all six of our sons, our son-in-law, and our grandsons were sitting together on an outcropping of rocks. My oldest son was teaching. As my wife, Merlene, saw this group of Aaronic and Melchizedek Priesthood holders, all six sons and her son-in-law Eagle Scouts, the oldest grandsons Eagle Scouts, the others deeply involved in Scouting, she said to me, "I have never been more grateful or pleased in my life for what you have done for our sons and family." I thought: *I owe it all to a great Scoutmaster who was a model of living in all dimensions of life.*

Let me conclude this chapter with a passage of scripture—the 7th chapter of Moses, verses 48–49: "And it came to pass that Enoch looked upon the earth; and he heard a voice from the bowels thereof, saying: Wo, wo is me, the mother of men; I am pained, I am weary, because of the wickedness of my children. When shall I rest, and be cleansed from the filthiness which is gone forth out of me? When will my Creator sanctify me, that I may rest, and righteousness for a season abide upon my face? And when Enoch heard the earth mourn, he wept, and cried unto the Lord, saying: O Lord, wilt thou not have compassion upon the earth?"

Enoch asked the Lord two more times when the earth would rest, and then came this promise from the Lord: "The day shall come that the earth shall rest; . . . and righteousness will I send down out of heaven; and truth will I send out of the earth" (verses 61–62).

All that is grand and magnificent about this beautiful earth shouts its witness of the glories of nature and the handiwork of God. May we have appropriate reverence for all the creations around us and do our part to help our mother earth find peace and rest.

17

It's a Privilege to Serve a Mission

In a letter sent to all bishops and stake presidents in the Church, the First Presidency stated that "full-time missionary service is a privilege, not a right" (letter dated June 18, 1998). For those who qualify, a call to serve is issued through inspiration by the president of the Church. Well might a young man or young woman who has prepared properly for that moment feel that the Lord is speaking through His prophet today as He did to Thomas Marsh through the Prophet Joseph Smith: "Lift up your heart and rejoice, for the hour of your mission is come; and your tongue shall be loosed, and you shall declare glad tidings of great joy unto this generation" (D&C 31:3).

Youth, especially young men, need to prepare spiritually, physically, and mentally for a mission. It is a glorious work, but it *is* work. It will require digging deep down inside of oneself to stay clean and sweet, to be self-disciplined, and to meet the requirements. Let no one say that a mission is easy, but the young man who loves the Lord and has lived his life deserving a mission will find the joy the Lord promised: "If it so be that you should labor all your days in crying repentance unto this people, and bring, save it be one soul unto me, how great shall be your joy with him in the kingdom of my Father" (D&C 18:15).

Young men and young women who desire to serve need to understand the doctrine of missionary work. They need to be prepared to live a spartan life of dedication and service. As they labor diligently in the field, they will come to understand the supreme greatness and goodness of God. He rewards His laborers well. A mission is not a social experience. In their letter, the First Presidency also stated about a mission: "Its objective is not primarily the personal development of an individual missionary, although righteous service invariably produces that result."

Many of you who are now leading and influencing youth will remember Elder Sterling W. Sill. After Elder Sill had been made an emeritus General Authority, I picked him up every Thursday for meetings of the Quorum of the Seventy. I did this for nearly five years. How his great mind blessed me! I would ponder before I picked him up about one question I could ask him, and usually it took the time from his home to the office to answer that question. One morning I asked him about his mission and how he was able to go since he came from a large family. He told me the following great story about that time in his life.

The year before he was old enough to go on a mission, he went to the bank and borrowed enough money for seed for sugar beets. He rented a field, plowed the ground, prepared the soil, and planted sugar beets (I believe it was about five acres). He watered, weeded, and thinned the beets as they grew. He knew that if the price stayed at $30 a ton, he would have enough money for his two-and-a-half-year mission. When harvest time came, he worked long hard hours harvesting the beets and getting them to the sugar factory. That year the price of sugar beets plummeted to $5 a ton! Young Sterling was devastated. He barely earned enough money back to pay off the loan. That fall, as the missionaries who had been called on missions went down to the railroad depot to depart, Elder Sill went with them. He had no money to pay for his mission. Most of the young men's fathers and families paid for their missions; a few had saved their own money.

As family and friends stood at the depot while the missionaries said their good-byes and boarded the train, everyone spontaneously broke into singing "God Be with You Till We Meet Again." Elder Sill said: "As the train pulled away from the station while the Saints sang and the missionaries waved good-bye, I thought my heart would break." He went out behind the station, sat down against the wall, and, in his own words, "cried like a baby." He said, "I would have *walked* all the way to Georgia if I could have gone on a mission."

The next spring he borrowed money again. He prepared the field, planted sugar beets, and worked through spring, summer, and fall. When harvest time came he loaded the sugar beets on wagon after wagon and hauled them to the factory. That year the market had changed, and he got between $25 and $30 a ton for his beets. It was enough to go on a mission. He submitted his papers and a short time later was called to serve in the Southern States. I remember glancing at Elder Sill as he recounted this experience. He had tears in his eyes, and he choked back the emotion several times. I too was moved to tears hearing of this great experience. No one could suppose that he was not a hard-working, great missionary. Also, you can imagine that Elder Sill felt it a wonderful privilege to serve a mission.

As a young man I remember reading and hearing about Elder Matthew Cowley's experiences with the Maori people in New Zealand. Immediately I had a desire to serve a mission in New Zealand, or at least the islands of the sea. I heard Elder Cowley tell about testimony meetings with the missionaries that lasted six and eight hours. I thought, "I would give anything to have those kinds of experiences." I went to the bishop and asked if I could go on a mission. It was during the Korean War, and they were taking only one missionary per ward per year. The bishop told me I would have to wait my turn in terms of seniority. We had a large ward, and about a dozen priests were older than I was and would turn 20 before I did. I remember thinking as Joe Brooks left for his mission from our ward, I would have given all I had to go. I believe I felt as Sterling Sill felt.

The young man who understands the privilege extended to him when he receives a mission call will be a marvelous missionary. Attitude is so important as one prepares for a mission. For years I have heard that 85 percent of all success is due to attitude. Attitude *is* important and is surely reflected in the way one serves. I believe that our attitude toward missionary service is a direct reflection of how much we love God and His Only Begotten Son. When we reverence Their holy names we will want to please Them through our service.

Worthiness is essential if a missionary is to have the Spirit with him. Occasionally a young man will commit a transgression so serious that it might delay or eliminate his opportunity for missionary service. Some young men who are spiritually inexperienced may think they can lie to a bishop or stake president to get into the mission field and then confess and repent while serving. Teach our young men that possible embarrassment and humiliation of being sent home shortly after they arrive in the mission field can be expected if they try such a thing. The best place to discuss worthiness issues is in the bishop's office before an application to serve has even been submitted. The bishop will then consult with the stake president and outline a course of action to prepare a young man for a mission or, if necessary, to redirect his life into another dimension of spiritual activity in the Church. Hopefully we can help prospective missionaries avoid these consequences. To be sent home shortly after leaving to serve hurts parents deeply, gives great concern to the bishop and stake president, and sets a poor example for future missionaries in the ward. Teach the young men and young women to do the courageous thing by dealing with any worthiness problems early on in their interviews with their bishop.

In a recent leadership meeting for General Authorities, Elder Joseph B. Wirthlin taught that a missionary should adopt the spirit that his mission belongs to the Lord. In our training of young men, we have all of the Aaronic Priesthood years to prepare for missions. As young men grow older and closer to missionary age, the training should intensify. It is thrilling to talk about missionary work. Young men love to hear others talk about their missions.

The following preparation can assist dramatically in intensifying the desire for young men to serve missions:

1. Help them to understand the doctrine of the Atonement as taught in the scriptures. As they understand this great principle, they will come to love and worship the Savior more. Understanding the doctrine of the Atonement will change their behavior. It will change their values and secure them to the gospel. Personalize the Atonement by showing what it has meant in your life. Faith in Christ and His Atonement is the supreme motivation. Abraham Maslow in his hierarchy of needs suggests that self-actualization is the pinnacle of motivators. This may be

true outside religion, but in the lives of Christians the world over it is faith in Christ.

2. Spiritual preparation is essential for every missionary: praying, studying the scriptures, attending church, fulfilling his or her duty, and maintaining moral purity and physical standards such as obeying the Word of Wisdom. To be spiritually prepared is to have a giant head start over those who do not when one enters the mission field.

3. Work is essential. Missionary service is hard work—mentally, spiritually, and physically. It is demanding. Every laborer knows that work requires discipline. Teach our youth to look for things that need to be done and then to do them. Even youth who have never worked outside the home can be taught the discipline of work by looking for things that need to be done. What if a young man or woman decided to see how much work there was around the house and systematically did it! Let's list a few chores that he or she might find: mow and edge the lawn, plant and care for vegetable and flower gardens, clean the garage, and organize tools; repair doors, screens, electrical plugs, sprinklers, and fences; paint sidings, fences, trim, the garage, and outdoor furniture; wash and iron the clothes; scrub and clean the floors, windows, basins, toilets, tub, and showers; wash the dishes, clear the table, prepare meals; drive the younger children to meetings, games, piano lessons; go grocery shopping; vacuum floors, sweep walks; care for pets; and so on.

Can you see the opportunities parents have available for training their children? If the older young men in the family knew that all of the work they were doing was in preparation for a mission, it would become a glory and not drudgery. Mental work requires even more discipline. Young people can study the scriptures, read great literature, and memorize poetry, scriptures, inspirational sayings, even the missionary discussions. Again, it will not be drudgery if they understand it is part of missionary preparation.

All work, mental and physical, builds character, stability, confidence, and self-esteem. Work is a marvelous part of life; it is fulfilling and rewarding. Wilfred Petersen, in his *Art of Living* series, made the following observation: "A master at the art of living makes no distinction between his work and his play, his labor and his leisure, his mind and his body, his education and his recreation, his love and his religion. He hardly knows which is which. He simply pursues with excellence what he is about and leaves others to determine whether he is working or playing. He, himself, always knows he is doing both."

Possibly the hardest work in the world is being lazy. Time moves so slowly—a second, a minute, an hour—that life simply drags by. Those who avoid work carry the heavy weight of nonperformance and dullness of character; they most often find themselves depressed. Laziness becomes a way of life and saps the manhood or womanhood out of the soul. To work is to save oneself, to bring credit for achievement, to earn one's way, and to fill a role in the community. Also, the person who knows hard work is usually blessed with hard sleep. Our youth need to know that you have to earn deep, sweet, peaceful, repairing sleep.

In addition to the previous three skills, teach our youth the importance of learning to work with people. Social skills can be developed, and they are vital. Teach them how to shake hands firmly and warmly while looking the other person in the eye. People respond when we are interested in them. King Lamoni responded to Ammon because Ammon wanted first to serve and please the king.

François René de Chateaubriand gave the history of man in a sentence: "In the days of service all things are founded; in the days of special privilege they deteriorate; and in the days of vanity they are destroyed."

Service is one way we prove our worth in the human race. It requires desire, time, and effort, but it is one of the great things people with people skills do. They want to bless the lives of all they meet. People skills can be developed and are invaluable once mastered.

Years ago I memorized a little poem by an unknown author:

> My life shall touch a hundred lives
> before this day is done;
> Make countless markers of good will
> before the setting sun.
> This is the thought I always think
> the prayer I always pray—
> Lord let my life bless every life
> it touches day by day.

The more we try to bless the lives of others, the more our own lives are blessed. One word of caution: develop your people skills for the purpose of serving your fellowmen, not for manipulating people. The service you render should not be self-serving.

As I think of Elder Sill's experience with the sugar beets and my own with the Korean War, the thought has come to me from time to time: what if conditions were to again change so that only a relatively few young men had the privilege of serving a mission? As we climb toward 75,000, 100,000, 500,000 missionary-age young men, we may not be able to call every young man on a mission because of conditions in the world or the numbers of young men available. Then I think we will begin to understand again what a privilege it is to serve a mission. Perhaps then only those who have truly prepared themselves, have been chaste, have desired a mission with all their hearts, and have prayed in the might of their souls for the privilege will be blessed to serve.

Whether that situation ever becomes a reality or not, we need every young man to consider that being called on a mission is a great privilege. Teach our youth to follow the Master, who alone can bring salvation to their souls. Help them to prepare well for that wonderful privilege we call full-time missionary service.

PART

4

....

LEADING
IN CHARACTER

18

Some Things Never Change

I first met George Eason when I was called to serve on the high council in the Salt Lake Valley View Stake. President Rex C. Reeve was the stake president, and his counselors were Wilford Edman and Allen Swan. I think that President Edman, who traveled a great deal, never missed a high council meeting. I heard tales of him flying from his company meetings in Florida back to Salt Lake City for high council meetings and then returning to his business meetings in Florida. In addition to our standard high council meetings in which we conducted the regular stake business, once a month we would meet early on a Sunday morning for a special spiritual meeting.

George Eason was one of the outstanding men on the high council. Although I do not recall precisely, I believe that he spoke to us one Sunday morning during our spiritual meeting. He told us that when he was a young man, about 12 as I recall, his mother and he moved to a community in California where there was no ward or branch of the Church. However, George's mother thought they should go to church every week, so they selected a nearby Protestant congregation and attended there for the next two or three years. Every Sunday George and his mother walked down to the church and then home again when the meeting was over.

One afternoon when George came home from school, his mother

came running to him as he entered the door. She had tears glistening in her eyes. She said, "Guess what, George! The Church has organized a branch here. Come and meet the new branch president. His mother then led him into the living room. There stood a relatively young man dressed in a suit. He introduced himself to George and shook his hand warmly. Then he said, "George, you are the only Aaronic Priesthood holder in our branch. We need you. We are going to use you and depend on you. You will be a great asset to the branch."

George said, "Hold on, I believe the Mormon Church is the true church, but all of my friends go to another church, and that is where I intend to go." His mother urged him, as did the branch president, but George was resistant and said he intended to go to church where his friends were. His mother did not force him.

Over the next few weeks and months, George would often round a corner and run into the branch president. He would often ask George if he would like to go to the drugstore for an ice cream soda. Sometimes they would just bump into each other, but always the branch president would walk with him wherever he was going. George said, "I can't tell you how often we just ran into each other. We became very good friends, and always he would let me know I was wanted and needed over at the branch. As I recall, the branch rented a Seventh-Day Adventist church building on Sunday. Every Sunday morning George's mother would get ready for church and walk down to her meeting, and George would get ready and walk to the Protestant church.

George related that one Sunday after the Protestant service, while he and a group of his friends were standing on the steps leading down from the church, the minister came out of the building dressed in all his ministerial robes. He came up to the group of young men and shook hands with each one. When he got to George, he looked at him for a long moment and then asked, "What is your name?" "It's George Eason, sir." The minister then said, "You must be new here; I don't believe I have seen you here before. Is this your first time?" George replied, "No, it isn't my first time, but it is my *last* time."

George then left the church and walked the few blocks to where the Latter-day Saints were meeting. He went through the doors into the foyer. He spotted a seat on the back row. The meeting was in progress, and George sat down and looked at the stand. His eyes met the branch president's eyes. He said, "I saw tears begin to glisten in his eyes. I knew he loved me, wanted me there, and cared about me." I only heard George tell this story once, but I have never forgotten it in the approximately 37 years since I first heard it.

In the Lord's affairs it will always be important for youth to have a bishop or adviser who loves and cares for them. A caring adviser is extremely important in activating or keep active the young people he or she is called to serve.

Working with youth will always require time. During the time I served in the General Presidency of the Young Men, I taught priesthood leaders the essentials in calling men to work with the Aaronic Priesthood. I called it my "Four T Talk."

The first T is for *testimony*. Testimony is more important than Scouting skills, personality, or age. The leader with a deep, abiding, and firm testimony has his or her calling in perspective. Such a leader knows that the most important thing in his or her calling is to help the young men or young women grow spiritually, to help strengthen their testimonies, and to increase their love for the Lord and His leaders.

The second T is for *training*. President David O. McKay taught that there is no greater work in this world than the training of a human soul. Competence in a call is essential. Most people are not talented enough to fill their calling by the "seat of their pants." When a leader is trained and prepared, it shows. It makes a statement, letting the youth know that they are important enough that leading and teaching them requires preparation. They know who is not prepared, and they soon get the message.

The third T is for *time*. When a leader is called to work with youth, he or she must have available time—not just for meetings but also for individual contact; time to go to sports competitions, debates, and recitals; and time for ward or stake sports, camping, or other special activities. It isn't a one-day-a-week job. Recently my wife spoke to a group of wives of stake and mission presidents. She related that just after we were married, I was called to be the Scoutmaster. She remembers how demanding the calling was.

She told about our first Christmas. She was expecting our first child, and we were both sound asleep. About 6:00 or 6:30 A.M., our doorbell rang. I got up, slipped on a pair of pants, and went to the door. There was one of my Scouts. He had gotten Scouting equipment for Christmas and wanted to share his joy with his Scoutmaster! My wife said, "I watched all this and thought, *Merlene, you had better get used to the idea, because this is the way it is going to be in your marriage, so there is no use resenting it or making a fuss about it.*" It does take time to work with the youth.

The next and final *T* is for *tenure*. Tenure is important to growth. Constant turnover in teachers or advisers shouts a loud, clear message that every other calling is more important than working with youth. When I was a young man we were transferred to Boise. Our bishop, Floyd Fletcher, called me to be the priests quorum adviser. What a youth-oriented bishop! He was terrific, as were his counselors, Gene Carter and Merlyn Olsen. I had 23 boys in the quorum. Two were in the military, and I had never met them. I wrote but never got a response. Of the other 21, 19 were Individual Award achievers (a special award for Aaronic Priesthood in that day), and 13 were 100 percent attendees. We had a great quorum. To this day I love those young men. We had a reunion a few years ago, and most all of them came to Boise, Idaho, to attend. I think only two or three were not able to come. They came from Colorado, Utah, California, and all across Idaho. We had a glorious time. I believe they are all grandparents now!

Dennis Flake was in our stake presidency. His son was in our priests quorum, and later his son Lawrence Flake came into the quorum. President Flake told me that the stake president wanted to call me to the high council but that he persuaded the stake president that I was doing more good where I was. Later he told me that the stake mission president wanted me for a counselor, but he again felt impressed to leave me where I was. Tenure is a critical issue. There is wisdom in leaving a man or woman in the calling long enough to be trained, to get to know the needs and interests of every young person, and to grow together. However, if a leader does not like working with youth and cannot truly love and serve them, I always suggest that the tenure should be very short.

There are two chapters in Ezekiel that let us know about the Lord's concern for his sheep. Consider carefully this warning voice:

"Son of man, speak to the children of thy people, and say unto them, When I bring the sword upon a land, if the people of the land take a man of their coasts, and set him for their watchman:

"If when he seeth the sword come upon the land, he blow the trumpet, and warn the people;

"Then whosoever heareth the sound of the trumpet, and taketh not warning; if the sword come, and take him away, his blood shall be upon his own head.

"He heard the sound of the trumpet, and took not warning; his blood shall be upon him. But he that taketh warning shall deliver his soul.

"But if the watchman see the sword come, and blow not the trumpet, and the people be not warned; if the sword come, and take any person from among them, he is taken away in his iniquity; but his blood will I require at the watchman's hand.

"So thou, O son of man, I have set thee a watchman unto the house of Israel; therefore thou shalt hear the word at my mouth, and warn them from me.

"When I say unto the wicked, O wicked man, thou shalt surely die; if thou dost not speak to warn the wicked from his way, that wicked man shall die in his iniquity; but his blood will I require at thine hand. . . .

"Say unto them, As I live, saith the Lord God, I have no pleasure in the death of the wicked; but that the wicked turn from his way and live: turn ye, turn ye from your evil ways; for why will ye die, O house of Israel?" (Ezekiel 33:2–8, 11).

Now consider these words from chapter 34: "Son of man, prophesy against the shepherds of Israel, prophesy, and say unto them, Thus saith the Lord God unto the shepherds; Woe be to the shepherds of Israel that do feed themselves! Should not the shepherds feed the flocks?

"Ye eat the fat, and ye clothe you with the wool, ye kill them that are fed: but ye feed not the flock.

"The diseased have ye not strengthened, neither have ye healed that which was sick, neither have ye bound up that which was broken, neither have ye brought again that which was driven away, neither have ye sought that which was lost: but with force and with cruelty have ye ruled them" (verses 2–4).

Then come the most lonely words in all of the Old Testament: "My sheep wandered through all the mountains, and upon every high hill: yea, my flock was scattered upon all the face of the earth, and none did search or seek after them" (verse 6).

Fortunately, parents and leaders are not alone in their efforts to care for the Lord's flocks. Note His comforting words as recorded in verses 11–15:

"For thus saith the Lord God; Behold, I, even I, will both search my sheep, and seek them out.

"As a shepherd seeketh out his flock in the day that he is among his sheep that are scattered; so will I seek out my sheep, and will deliver them out of all places where they have been scattered in the cloudy and dark day.

"And I will bring them out from the people, and gather them from the countries, and will bring them to their own land, and feed them upon the mountains of Israel by the rivers, and in all the inhabited places of the country.

"I will feed them in a good pasture, and upon the high mountains of Israel shall their fold be: there shall they lie in a good fold, and in a fat pasture shall they feed upon the mountains of Israel.

"I will feed my flock, and I will cause them to lie down, saith the Lord God."

Fortunately for George Eason and many, many others like him, the Lord does seek out his lost sheep, often working through leaders like the young branch president serving in George's obscure branch, a leader not content to lose one of his flock.

René de Chardin said:

> Someday after we have mastered the winds,
> the waves, the tides, and gravity,
> we will harness for God the energies of love
> and then, for the second time in the history of the world,
> Man will have discovered fire.

19

Teach Youth to Be Kind

All of us know people who are kind. A kind person is friendly, gentle, and benevolent. In the second chapter of Joel we read this description of the Lord: "He is gracious and merciful . . . and of great kindness" (verse 13). What a wonderful world this would be if everyone would just be gracious to each other, if they would be "merciful . . . and of great kindness." Every principle of the gospel teaches us to be loving and forgiving. When we do these things we are kind. The *Oxford Dictionary* defines gracious living as an "elegant way of life." One who is gracious is kind, merciful, and benign; one who is benign is gentle, mild, and kind.

After David sinned with Bathsheba, he pleaded with the Lord: "Have mercy upon me, O God, according to thy lovingkindness: according unto the multitude of thy tender mercies" (Psalm 51:1). David knew the Lord and described Him as we know Him. In spite of his serious transgressions, he knew he could—and should—turn to the Lord, who is kind.

Proverbs 19:22 states, "The desire of a man is his kindness." And Mormon reminds us that "charity suffereth long, and is kind" (Moroni 7:45). A kind person, then, is benevolent, gentle, gracious, charitable, and merciful, has an elegant way of life and is benign. As we think of such a description, we have images come to mind of people who are kind. For example, think about the individuals who make up the First Presidency of our church. President Hinckley's ministry is based on kindness. He has traveled up and down, back and forth across this great world. He knows what it means for people to be able to see and hear the prophet. It doesn't matter how tired or exhausted he may become, he continues traveling to distant parts of the earth.

In his great kindness he has sought direction from the Lord regarding the members of the Church and their access to holy temples. In turn, the Lord has instructed his prophet to build temples close to the people. Temples are so important in this great work. President Howard W. Hunter called going to the temple "our ultimate, earthly goal and the supreme mortal experience" (*Ensign,* Feb. 1995, p. 5). That is why President Hinckley wants to have temples near the people. It is certainly a kind and charitable thing to do. He is kind when he talks about the youth: there is no harshness, only gratitude for this wonderful generation who are excelling all other generations. There is much of solicitude and concern over those who are straying. And finally, I offer my personal witness of President Hinckley's kindness to the General Authorities.

President Monson's concern for the widow, the orphan, and the poor and needy are constant. He loves the little children and is a champion for the youth. His energies and efforts for the Scouting movement the world over are an expression of his kindness for the youth of the world. Every talk he gives at general conference is imbued with loving kindness through beautiful stories, examples, and an understanding of the scriptures that teach us to care and to be charitable. No mortal knows how many times his loving, kind spirit has taken him to the hospital to bless the sick and suffering. He is a good and humble prophet of God.

President James E. Faust is a thoughtful man. He is considerate about women's issues, especially how men treat their wives and children. I have never heard that President Faust has raised his voice or been critical of anyone. I am certain he is aware of our weaknesses, but he has never been anything but kind. He is a man filled with gratitude. He is so appreciative of anything that is done for him or for the Church. He has the gentle spirit of a Howard W. Hunter and the thoroughness of a J. Reuben Clark. He stands tall in the corner of the underdog. He is fair, and, as all the General Authorities know, you can trust your reputation and name with him.

Many years ago we lived in a ward where Paul Pehrson was bishop. There could hardly have been a kinder man alive. A woman in the neighborhood who had two children was in serious financial straits. There was no father in the home. Her son was in his mid-teens. He played the piano with a special God-given talent and a love for the instrument. It helped his self-esteem to excel at something that the other youth admired. One year financial conditions were so severe that this good mother had to sell the piano to make ends meet. It was, I am sure, one of the most difficult things she ever had to do in her life, knowing what it meant to her son. You can imagine the heaviness of heart, almost to breaking, every time she thought of the loss her son felt over the piano. That Christmas a beautiful piano was delivered to their home—a gift to the son from some unknown benefactor. I don't know if the family ever did find out who gave them the piano, but I suppose if they had thought, "Who is the kindest man we know?" they would have known it was Bishop Paul Pehrson.

Kindness is being able to see things that many do not see. A kind person will see and feel the suffering of others, even those whom he or she does not know. Quite often I sit in airports and watch people. My heart aches at some of the things I see. A mother and child or children sit waiting for the father's plane to arrive. They are anxious; they watch excitedly; you can feel the anticipation. Finally when the husband and father arrives, their eyes light up with joy. I have often seen some men's response—more often than not they will come off the plane seemingly preoccupied, give a half-hearted smile, and, with little show of affection, start walking toward the exit. I hurt inside. Such apparent lack of feeling is not only *not kind,* it is many times *unkind.* I want to go up to such a man and say, *"Hug your children! Kiss your wife! Be as excited to see them as they are to see you!"*

We recently had a couple serving in our area office in Australia. Brother Joseph Smith and his wife live in Idaho. He was not feeling well when he left after his mission. When he arrived home they discovered he had cancer. His stomach and the glands around the stomach have all been removed. He is now receiving chemotherapy.

I called the family while we were in Salt Lake City for general conference, and I share here some of what they related to me. After my call at conference time, Brother Smith had surgery to remove his stomach.

My wife urged me several times to call him from Australia. Finally I called. When he answered, I asked, "How are you feeling? How are you doing?" With his always upbeat attitude, even with an almost cheery ring to his voice, he responded, "This has been the hardest two months in my life, and the last three weeks have been especially difficult. The last three days have been the worst experience of my life. Your call is more important to me than you will ever know." We talked for a time, and after I hung up I sat and thought about this wonderfully good man who was suffering so much, and I became very emotional. When I tried to tell my wife about what the phone call meant to him, I could hardly speak. She understood, for she had felt, through her kindness, that a phone call would help.

We live in a time of cruelty. Movies have scenes of five- and six-year-old children bad-mouthing their parents, and other children defying, threatening, swearing in a vulgar way, and even terrifying parents! Our youth are exposed to mothers who counsel their teenage youth to be involved in "safe sex" with no discussion or concern about morality or chastity! We see children shooting children and gangs assaulting individuals, with no conscience. There is a social sickness that is creating a terrible stench, and the sickness is spreading and attacking all ages. As leaders of youth, we must stand strong—alone if necessary. Someone said, "Though argument does not change belief, the lack of it destroys belief." Also, I believe that when we resist correcting someone who needs to be corrected, it is because we are more interested in ourselves than we are in building the kingdom.

Often we would rather not confront a person or a situation because we think people may like us less. This is a disservice, not only to the member but also to the Church. We all need to be corrected regularly. Certain conduct may be unacceptable to the Lord, unacceptable in our home, unacceptable at school, or unacceptable in our relationships with others. Regardless of how many people or how great a percentage of the nation may choose to be vulgar, irresponsible, mean, dangerous, obnoxious, lewd, ill-tempered, spoiled, dishonest, indulgent, tattooed, excessively bejeweled, or criminal—despite all this, it is still unacceptable conduct in the eyes of God and of all good men and women.

We must teach our youth that kindness is its own reward. I just learned of a visiting teacher who regularly visits a homebound sister.

One day the ward Relief Society president said to her, "I am constantly hearing things about you. I dropped in on our homebound sister, as I do often. My whole intention was just to visit with her (which, I might add, is a wonderful reason). She told me, 'Sister —————— visits me often. She is my visiting teacher. During each visit she always asks if there is something she can do for me—"perhaps something you would like to do if you were up and around?" she often says. I told her, "I would like to empty all my waste baskets, and I wish I could change the bed pan." My visiting teacher does this. She always asks how she can help.'"

The Relief Society president then asked this visiting teacher, "How did you get her to let you do that?" The response was, "I just visited her often. We are very good friends. She trusts me and knows I will not find fault, and she knows I am sincere about wanting to help. You have to build the relationship of trust." This sweet visiting teacher would never have let anyone know what she had done. She simply reported that visiting teaching was getting done. That great method of teaching kindness will always be a fine example.

For me, watching kindness in action is an emotional experience. I feel it deeply when I watch a parent, teacher, coach, or friend doing a kind thing for someone else. People are always doing wonderfully kind things for us in our callings as General Authorities. I am always appreciative, but I know as you do that sometimes it is done primarily because of the callings we have. Then there are others who do kind things for Vaughn Featherstone—and not because he is a General Authority. You know who these people are in your life, and I know who they are in mine.

A young man who was running for senior class president was one day waiting in the high school cafeteria. Another female student, one of the less popular ones, tripped and fell into her food tray. The fall was humiliating and apparently made some clatter that attracted attention. Some students laughed, and others made negative and sneering comments. The young man who was running for senior class president went to her, helped her up, brushed away the food, and tried to remove the stains. He then gave her his lunch money and said, "Go get yourself another tray of food. I will clean this up." She left the humiliating mess, which was cleared up quickly. The father of the boy heard about this from someone else. His son had not mentioned it—he just did a kind thing for an embarrassed girl. The father said, "I would rather have had my son do what he did than be elected senior class president." Interestingly enough, this fine young man *was* elected senior class president. He went on to serve a mission and is now a young bishop.

Kind people see the needs of the lonely, the heartsick, the poor, those with low self-esteem, the awkward, the embarrassed, the less fortunate, and a multitude of others. Sometimes beautiful people can be as lonely as those who may be less attractive. The kind person is an aware person. He or she constantly watches for anyone who needs a lift or a kind word.

I was privileged to be invited to write a chapter in a book entitled *Turning Points.* The objective was to share with readers the different turning points in the lives of those who were invited to contribute. After the book was published, I read it thoroughly and was deeply impressed. I hope someday there will further volumes as leaders emerge! It was a learning experience to read of the turning points in other people's lives. Russell M. Nelson was a contributor. I would like to quote a small part from his chapter:

"I had not concerned myself much with the miracle of our own endowment of the physical body we possess.

"I looked at natural human heart valves with a new sense of wonder. Four tiny valves open and close over a hundred thousand times a day, over thirty-six million times a year, serving without our awareness or gratitude. They are soft and billowy as a parachute, yet tough as sinew. To this date, man has not been able to create such a material, one that can fold and unfold that frequently without stress-fatigue and ultimate fracture.

"The heart each day pumps enough blood to fill a two-thousand gallon tank car, and it performs work equivalent to lifting a 150-pound person to the top of the Empire State Building, while consuming only about four watts of energy, less than the dimmest light bulb.

"At the crest of the heart is an electrical transmitting center that sends signals down special lines that cause millions of muscle fibers to beat together with a synchronized response that would be the envy of any conductor of a symphony orchestra.

"I began to fathom the real meaning of the scriptural passage I had previously glossed over, 'For the *power* is in them' (D&C 58:28, italics added). While considering protective mechanisms, I realized that one of the most marvelous is the skin, the most rugged yet sensitive cover one could imagine.

"We could, if we had to, get along without our arms, legs, eyes, or ears; we could possibly even survive with somebody else's heart or kidneys. But without this cloak in which we all find ourselves, our skin, we would die. If a large enough portion of his skin is destroyed, man cannot live" ("A Mighty Change," *Turning Points* [Salt Lake City: Bookcraft, 1981]).

Not long ago, during lunch in the General Authority lunchroom, I asked Elder Nelson about the book and his chapter. Then I said, "Elder Nelson, I know adrenaline is a powerful thing. I have read over the years of men and women performing unbelievable acts—a woman in her seventies lifting the back of a car off a child, a man lifting a car off someone who was trapped, and mothers performing herculean feats to save their children." I asked, "Is adrenaline that powerful?" He responded that it was very powerful, but then he taught me something I believe with all my heart. He said, "Do you know why certain people can do such things? It is because of their spirit." There are those who have such spirits—you know them, and so do I.

The scriptures bear this out: "All spirit is matter, but it is more fine or pure" (D&C 131:7). It is their spirit that enables them to do such incredible feats, and I believe they have special spirits because they are kind. Kind people hurt when other people suffer.

Help our youth to understand that the supreme example of kindness is the Master. Jesus Christ is not only the author of charity, but charity is described as His pure love. The Lord revealed to the Prophet Joseph Smith, "And now the year of my redeemed is come; and they shall mention the loving kindness of their Lord, and all that he has bestowed upon them according to his goodness, and according to his loving kindness, forever and ever" (D&C 133:52). Those who are kind are good.

"And above all things have fervent charity among yourselves: for charity shall cover the multitude of sins" (1 Peter 4:8). As I have discussed in my last two books, the Atonement covers the innocent as well as the guilty. Often the innocent suffer far, far more than those who sin or transgress. It would not be just or kind if the Atonement covered only the perpetrator: what about the innocent victim? According to God's kindness and His supreme goodness, the innocent can find peace, relief, and freedom from suffering and pain.

Kindness will change lives. Youth who will make an effort to become kind will find a richness of life, a deep penetrating joy, and a spiritual affirmation of their own worth from God.

20

"Good Kid" Tools

At about age 18, I came out of my girlfriend's home one day (she was the girl I eventually married). Her family had a number of rose-bushes lining the fence at the side of their driveway. Nearly half a century later, I can still recall vividly as I walked over to one of the rosebushes. The flowers were a deep, rich red. I broke the stem off and smelled the rose. The fragrance was wonderful.

Then I *looked* at a rose for the first time in my life.

I had picked dozens and dozens of roses over the years, smelled them, and cast them away—the way most children and youth handle flowers. I remember admiring them, loving the smell, and then just as quickly discarding them. This day was different. I looked at the rose deeply. I saw each petal, seemingly dusted with some heavenly sub-stance, beautiful beyond words. Involuntarily tears came. I was looking at something so beautiful that it touched my soul, and the tears gath-ered in my eyes.

Slowly I began the walk toward home. I was so caught up in this experience, but I did not realize I was having a *spiritual experience* resulting from having looked at a rose. I thought about a Creator who could create something so beautiful. I was touched by the creation but moved far more deeply by the Creator. Since then, roses have been among my favorite flowers. A few short years ago I wrote a poem about roses. Though it doesn't seem to fit in this book, it will have a place in my heart forever. And it all germinated from that one special experience.

As the years have passed since that day in my girlfriend's driveway, I have had equally and sometimes more thrilling experiences by listening to music or seeing a magnificent painting. I have been moved to tears by great orators, beautiful poetry, and couples skating flawlessly in sweeping rhythmic grace that can nearly take your breath away.

I recall a story I shared years ago in one of my books. In a major American city a museum had procured a world-renowned piece of art to put on public display for several weeks. It was properly advertised, and people came in great numbers to see this masterpiece, just for a few small moments. One man stood in a long line that went out the front door, down the street, and around the corner. He waited for several hours. At last it was his turn, and he stood in front of this masterful work of art. He looked at it long and hard, from every angle. Finally, he turned to the guard who was on duty to protect this great masterpiece and said, "I don't see anything special." The guard responded, "But don't you wish you could?"

I believe it is the spiritual dimension of our lives that sees the elegance, the eloquence, the beautiful, and the noble in music, art, speech, and dance.

Something of the divine is in those who see the majesty in mountains and the glories in waterfalls, trees, shrubs, flowers, lakes, oceans, and meadows; animals, birds, and fish; the stars and moon, the clouds and sky, sunrises and sunsets, rivers and streams. Then there is the beauty in the soft skin of an infant, the trust of a child, the softness of rain, the sweetness of cleanliness, and the old man with calloused hands kneeling in church. Many there are who see the enormously beautiful and fragrant diversities of life.

Far greater are the number who will never see, know, or sense even remotely the awe of what I just described. They see only the traffic, smog, dirt, smoke, ugliness, and debased side of life. They hear only gossip and derogatory rumors. They feel only pain, sorrow, and fear.

Could you feel the transition from something rare and noble to something far less—in just one paragraph?

Youth need to be exposed to, be around, and associate with those souls who see the rare and beautiful. John Gardner in his book *Self-Renewal* states:

"Young people do not assimilate values of their group by learning words (truth, justice, etc.) and their definitions. They learn attitudes, habits, and ways of judging. They learn these in intensely personal transactions with their immediate family or associates. They learn them in the routines and crises of living, but they also learn them through songs, stories, drama, and games. They do not learn ethical principles; they emulate ethical or unethical people. They do not analyze or list the attributes they wish to develop; they identify with people who seem to have those attributes. That is why young people need models, both in their imaginative life and in their environment, models of what man at his best can be."

What John Gardner states is true. We have heard this counsel all of our lives from the Brethren. What a blessing when youth are exposed to persons with enlarged souls. Those who feel, sense, and become emotional, who cannot restrain tears from flowing while listening to a great musician, viewing a masterpiece of art, or observing anything uplifting—these are the examples to whom all youth need exposure.

Activities in the Church are God-inspired for a purpose, but they must be balanced. When youth see adults and Church leaders only in meetings, they are left to emulate the ways of the world in music, dance, drama, sports, outdoor life, athletics, social settings, politics, and so on. Again, Church activities do have a priesthood purpose. They provide proper masculine and feminine examples that are needed by today's youth. Our young men and young women have an abundance of energy. Activities provide opportunities for them in a controlled environment to see the right kinds of models of ethical and sportsmanlike conduct in the best setting. Bishops and counselors, advisers and parents do well to have the youth see them in various settings created by such activities.

It is interesting how much influence conscientious parents have on their children. But adding the influence of "third party" adult leaders who serve the youth increases our success dramatically.

In March 1995 the *Washington Times* published a revealing study involving more than 270,000 students, grades six to twelve. The research revealed "good kid tools," both external and internal. As you review the results of this study in the charts at the end of this chapter, consider the teachings of our Church leaders and the counsel relating to the family that we have received from them over the years.

The charts are self-explanatory. The first list of good kid tools is a list of external assets; the second lists internal assets. As in all such honest studies, the results vindicate the Church and what we counsel and train our youth to do.

You will note that these lists include characteristics and values that we want our children and youth to have. The Church and our youth advisers can lend a great support to the family, but there is no substitute for a conscientious father and mother who commit their all to bringing up a well-adjusted, honest, service- and work-oriented and testimony-filled family of children. Without such commitment, some of our children might be fortunate enough to be led to truly look at a rose and understand its rare qualities, but we leave so much to chance. With the dedication of loving parents and trusting leaders, children can learn to walk frequently in the rose gardens of life, drinking deeply from the wells of spiritual experience that God has placed all around us.

Each one on this earth is eternally unique, but we and our children must learn to recognize and develop that spark of the divine in us that enables us to become like our Heavenly Father. Those of us with a few years of experience have come to understand that there can be no more lofty goal in life than to teach our youth to "seek ye first the kingdom of God, and his righteousness," for successfully doing so brings the Lord's promise that "all else shall be given unto you" (see Matthew 6:33).

GOOD KID TOOLS

Teens need the following 30 "assets" in their lives to succeed, according to a book based on a Search Institute study of more than 270,000 students in grades six through 12.

External assets kids need:

1. Warm, caring family home.
2. Approachable parents.
3. Communicative parents.
4. Other approachable adults.
5. Other communicative adults.
6. Parental involvement in school.

7. Positive school climate.

8. Parental standards.

9. Parental discipline.

10. Parental monitoring.

11. Limits on away-from-home socializing.

12. Positive peer influences.

13. Music lessons.

14. Organized extracurricular activities.

15. Community activities.

16. Involvement with a faith community.

Internal assets kids need:

1. Desire to achieve.

2. Desire to advance educationally.

3. Desire for above average grades.

4. Self-discipline to do 6-plus hours of homework a week.

5. Desire to help people.

6. Global concern.

7. Empathy.

8. Sexual restraint.

9. Assertiveness skills.

10. Decision-making skills.

11. Friendship-making skills.

12. Planning skills.

13. Self-esteem.

14. Hope.

HOW MANY ASSETS DO MOST TEENS HAVE?

The Search Institute found that teens on average had 16 to 30 assets. Teens should have a minimum of 25 assets, researchers say—

Grade	Average number of assets
6	17.8
7	17.1
8	16.6
9	16.1
10	16.0
11	15.9
12	16.0

HOW DO ASSETS MAKE A DIFFERENCE?

Teens with the most "assets" seldom engage in risky behaviors.

	Alcohol use	Sexual activity	School failure	Depression and suicide	Antisocial behavior and violence
0–10	44%	52%	31%	42%	51%
11–20	23%	34%	13%	25%	29%
21–25	9%	17%	4%	11%	13%
26–30	3%	7%	1%	5%	6%

Number of assets

21

The Victory of Good over the Tyranny of Evil

For approximately 30 years I have subscribed to *Vital Speeches of the Year*. A truly enlightening publication, it shares what the publishers consider to be the vital speeches made by world business and political leaders, professors, religionists, and others. William Van Dusen Wishard included the following information in a speech: "INTEL is installing computers in the National labs capable of cracking speeds of one teraflop, or one trillion calculations a second. They're already planning for computers capable of 10, even 100, teraflops" (*Vital Speeches*, May 15, 1998, p. 458).

USA Today had this interesting observation: "In .0043 seconds (less than one two thousandths of a second) the entire works of William Shakespeare can be translated into 200 languages and be sent from New York to Omaha, Nebraska, without skipping a verse" (*USA Today*, April 8, 1998, p. 9).

Current optic transmission lines can carry 1 to 2 gigabits per second, and laboratories have achieved rates of 80 gigabits per second. Light travels six trillion miles in the time of one year. Transmitting with light waves at rates of one trillion bits per second, the Library of

Congress's entire 1991 collection of books, amounting to 25 terabits, could be transmitted in just over 5 minutes (512.5 seconds) (see *Vital Speeches,* 1998, p. 359).

Consider that a million seconds is 12 days; a billion seconds, 32 years; and a trillion seconds, 32,000 years. Imagine—if you could do a major calculation each second, it would take you 32,000 years to do a trillion such calculations. Now computers can do that many in a second. And soon, if projections are accurate, they will be able to do 100 trillion calculations a second.

Synthonics, an electronics company, has developed technology that was referred to in Provost Dennis O'Connor's column in the July 1998 issue of *Smithsonian Research* reports: "Technological advances have revolutionized the way in which scholars and researchers can access and utilize the collections (Smithsonian Museum Collections). For example, an extraordinary new photographic imaging technique pioneered by Synthonics Technologies has recently captured objects from the Vidal collection (3,664 objects representing the arts, culture and history of Puerto Rico; donated by Tedoro Vidal of San Juan) in a most unprecedented and engaging fashion. While other graphic methods generate 2D representations of an object, this new technology produces an exact photo replica in 3 dimensions that can be viewed on a laptop computer."

We live in the day of the multifaceted uses of the laser, including but not limited to music, television, surgery, and warfare. Cellular phones are everywhere. Recently Elder Bruce C. Hafen was in Samoa and needed to call the office of the Quorum of the Twelve. He stepped outside the chapel and in a few moments was talking to an apostle in Salt Lake City. Telephone imaging allows you to see whom you are talking to, and hundreds of other truly incredible inventions and applications are coming in just the telephone industry.

Well, that is enough background to make a point: We live in an unusual day. Many of our youth have known only this high-tech computer age. It is their way of life. However, all the technological advances in the world cannot build character, integrity, and morality into the lives of our youth. President Kimball has talked about these technological advances as inspired for the use of the Lord's work; they surely can do that, and they will do more than we can now imagine. However, our youth need to be taught that they must live according to a certain set of high standards to have character, to be moral, and to develop a mind that can never be replaced by a machine.

When I wrote *A Generation of Excellence,* I did not have a chapter about computers, cellular phones, and other modern technology. It was not a problem then; however, today it offers a plethora of potential vices.

Imagine the marvels of the Worldwide Web and the Internet. Untold information, including genealogical data, is available at a second's request. Consider also those who have polluted the Internet with sex, child pornography, and other evils beyond belief, evils that can come right into a wonderful, spiritual Latter-day Saint family home by a few simple finger movements. There is so much information accessible on the Internet that youth could spend every minute they are awake on it. Many spend far, far too much time.

Recently I was in the home of a priesthood leader. He had two teenage sons. Their friends came over to visit each night I was there. I would not be exaggerating to suggest that they may have spent six hours each evening after school playing Nintendo. Some of your youth spend that much time on the computer. There are families whose children have phone bills of over a thousand dollars a month because they have called telephone numbers that access pornographic and sexual conversations. Consider how Elder Hafen was able to use the telephone, this marvelous invention; on the other hand, consider how easily children and youth can access filth.

We must stand in the breach and help our youth along. We need to appeal to them through their interests. We need to show by example what the well-balanced life is.

When we lock up our cultural halls and take the hoops off the outdoor basketball standards, we are by performance "excluding" our youth. Every poolhall, billiard parlor, nightclub, discotheque, gay bar, and other unsavory club has bright, attractive lights with doors wide open, and they use every method they can devise to appeal to our youth and young adults.

One father told his new General Authority son that he thought the meanest word in the English language was *exclude.* We ought to make it so easy and attractive for our youth to go to our cultural halls or parking lots to play basketball. We ought to keep new nets on the hoops with a few basketballs on hand, purchased out of budget funds. We ought to have teams organized and provide uniforms, referees, and wonderful leaders to be there with the youth. We ought to have drama, speech, and musical productions that appeal to our youth. Mutual ought to be the best night of the week for our youth, other than home evening. If it is planned and is exciting and stimulating, our youth will not want to miss. In fact, they will hardly be able to wait for the next Mutual night. Most youth enjoy being with good and interesting adults. They enjoy healthy and stimulating conversations.

One study showed that the thing that had the single greatest impact on the children in a family was the unplanned, unscheduled discussions in the home about the gospel. As a youth I loved to hear adults talking about gospel subjects, and I was thrilled at what I could learn.

A wonderful friend with whom I grew up was Robert Williams. He now lives in Hurricane, Utah. When he was a teenager, he was assigned to go home teaching with Brother Woodward, who was probably 75 to 80 years old. After going home teaching, Bob Williams would share with us what Brother Woodward taught his families. The first time I ever heard about the plan of salvation and the three degrees of glory was from Bob Williams, who shared with us what he learned by listening to Brother Woodward teach that message to his four or five families. I believed it then, and I believe it now. I remember the night Bob shared that with a group of teenage friends from the ward. I think we were all teachers in the Aaronic Priesthood. Youth love to hear adults talk about values, spiritual matters, and events. We can have a powerful influence for good if we think and communicate clearly.

Scouting is another healthy dimension of activity. It has a special attraction for most young men. Even the boys who do not care for Scouting will learn much by being registered in a good troop with a spiritual and trained Scout leader. Any young man in this world can learn much by memorizing, quoting weekly, and living the Scout Oath: "On my honor I will do my best to do my duty to God and my country and to obey the Scout law; to help other people at all times; to keep myself physically strong, mentally awake, and morally straight."

Wouldn't it be wonderful if every young man did his duty to God and his country? They would honor the flag and uphold the law; they would serve as the Master served; they would pray and be a wonderful example.

What a blessing is a young man who keeps the Scout Law: "A Scout is trustworthy, loyal, helpful, friendly, courteous, kind, obedient, cheerful, thrifty, brave, clean, and reverent." Those are qualities that will make a real man out of him.

What a blessing if a young man would "help other people at all times." You can imagine what would happen in his life if he did that. "To keep myself physically strong." Consider the result if young men and young women who sit at the computer or who play video games all day, who sit and watch television hours at a time, would commit to themselves to "keep myself physically strong." Physical health is important to their mortal welfare. And remember that to be "mentally awake" implies being alive, active, thoughtful, and clear thinking.

And being "morally straight" is simply the standard we should all live.

Every young man in the Church should subscribe 100 percent to this part of Scouting. Most youth love high adventure, backpacking, rappelling, river running, swimming, lifesaving, first aid, and such activities. Whenever I have heard parents say, "Well, my son doesn't like Scouting!" I always think, "Well, your son doesn't understand Scouting, or he has a poor Scoutmaster who is not carrying out the Scouting program." We now have six sons and one son-in-law, all of whom are Eagle Scouts. We have 24 grandsons, and 10 of these are Eagle Scouts. Imagine, Scouting offers more than 120 merit badges that lead in almost any worthy direction a young man could desire. Rank advancement develops needed lifelong skills that bless individuals and prepare them for great service in the Church and community. Any young man who will honestly consider the values and standards in the Scout Oath and Law, the physical and mental growth and development, the knowledge and skills gained, would certainly have to like Scouting. The great problem we have in Scouting is that we don't have spiritual, trained, tenured leaders who will love the young men, implement the program, and spend the time necessary to truly be a "Scout master." The title *Scoutmaster* implies that the leader is both a master at Scouting and a master with boys.

Scouting is one of the last few bastions holding on to morality, duty to God, ethics, and excellence. Scouting is not the enemy of the Church. Drugs, pornography, laziness, and indulgence are. Let's fight the real enemy and bless Scouting with all our efforts and in our prayers.

At the tomb of Robert F. Kennedy are these words:

> In our sleep, pain that cannot forget
> falls drop by drop upon the heart,
> and in our despair, against our wills
> comes wisdom through
> the awful grace of God.
> (Aeschylus.)

We may wake up one day with enough wisdom to support the causes that bless the lives of our youth. Scouting is one example, and another is activities. For a few members of the Church, criticism of welfare, Scouting, and activities is increasing. Remember, activities are not the enemy—they are essential to well-being and balance in the lives of the youth. What is a problem is having an excessive number of activities that require youth to be away from home too much. Think about wholesome sports in the Church (a family activity); a roadshow or drama production (a family activity); and a speech, music, or dance festival (all potential family activities).

With our youth, as well as with some adults, there is always a reason they give for not doing something, and then there is the *real* reason. For example, some of our youth say that they don't like seminary, Scouting, Mutual, and such activities because they doesn't interest them or they don't like the program or they don't have time. The *real* reason, most often, is that they are not willing to make a commitment or to discipline their lives. One of the major concerns with this generation is that we have not taught them the value in hard work and sacrificing for something.

Teach our youth to have balance in using the computer, watching TV, playing video games, and spending time on the phone. They need to allocate time for reading. Young people who read regularly will set a discipline in their lives that will bless them forever. They will be able to read the best thoughts from the best minds, and they can read them over and over again for comprehension.

C. S. Lewis wrote a marvelous book entitled *The Great Divorce*. In it he claimed that the wretched and miserable, through sympathy and pity, choose to hold hostage all those who surround them. That is, "because of your love and interest and ties that bind you to me, I will not let you be happy except on my terms. I will not let you be happy until I choose, because I am miserable. Because of your love for me and your concern you cannot really be happy as long as I am miserable, and thus your mercy will hold you hostage because of the great void in your life created by my misery."

Lewis clarifies this principle in these words: "Did you think joy was created to live always under that threat? Always defenseless against those who would rather be miserable than have their self-will crossed? For it was really misery. That you can still do. But you can no longer communicate your wretchedness. Everything becomes more and more itself. Here is joy that cannot be shaken. Our light can never swallow your darkness: but your darkness cannot now infect our light. No, no, no. Come to us. We will not go to you. Can you really have thought that love and joy would always be at the mercy of frowns and sighs? Did you know that they were stronger than their opposites?"

There is far too much suicide among the youth of the world. Somehow Satan puts deception into their minds so that they think: "I will get even with you. I will make you suffer the rest of your life blaming yourself for my death!" Many parents suffer just the way their child wanted them to. But this is spiritual immaturity. It would not be just to forever hold the innocent, loving parents or relatives hostage because the one who committed suicide had that as his or her objective. Remember, the Atonement covered the innocent as well as the transgressor and the guilty.

C. S. Lewis continues: "The demand of the loveless and the self imprisoned that they should be allowed to blackmail the universe; that till they consent to be happy (on their own terms) no one else shall taste joy; that theirs shall be the final power; that hell should be able to veto Heaven. . . ."

Lewis then responds to this approach: "It must be one way or the other. Either the day must come when joy prevails and all the makers of misery are no longer able to infect it; or else for ever and ever the makers of misery can destroy in others the happiness they reject for themselves. . . .

"It will not, at the cunning tears of hell, impose on good the tyranny of evil. Every disease that submits to cure shall be cured; but we will not call blue yellow to please those who insist on still having jaundice, nor make a midden [a dunghill] of the world's garden for the sake of one who cannot abide the smell of roses" ([New York: Macmillan, 1946], pp. 120–21).

We have some rebellious young men and women who make their homes into a living hell with their sour faces, negative attitudes, rebelliousness, temper tantrums, and selfishness. The only time they are happy at home is when their equally spoiled and selfish friends come to visit them. Their lives are out of control; they have no interest in following loving and wise counsel from the parents. They want only to decry perceived unfairness toward their spoiled, unmet desires.

Parents cannot allow this to happen. We do not have to react with contention and become as unhappy and miserable as these children are. We need to let them know they cannot and will not hold all other family members hostage because of their selfishness and immaturity. Our homes must be sweet, peaceful, loving homes in spite of those who rebel. The rest of the family deserves a warm, sweet home to which they can repair. We must sing, laugh, and play. We must study the scriptures and pray. We must express our love in words and hugs; if one of the family chooses to reject that, let it not affect and disease the rest of the family.

When we understand the great plan of happiness designed by our God, when we understand the glories of the telestial kingdom, it will be more beautiful than we could suppose. Every soul—those in the lower kingdoms and those in the celestial kingdom—will take joy fully at the glory and kingdom each one will be assigned. If some of our posterity reject a higher glory through their actions on earth, we will know that the loving kindness of God has rewarded them wonderfully for having kept their first estate. We cannot be held hostage by those of our posterity who fail, any more than God can be held hostage because a third part of His children chose to follow Lucifer.

Again, it would be spiritually immature to take the blame if we have done all we can and have been good parents, and yet our children commit suicide or rebel against God. That would not be just.

With all the modern technology available through computers, phones, and lasers, we must still remember that growth requires discipline, effort, thinking, and work. Computers can never provide a single person who walks on this earth with character, integrity, honesty, physical strength, love, and well-being. These will come only as we follow the teachings of the gospel. That is what we must teach our youth. We are truly free only when we are obedient. To be disobedient is to damn ourselves, to hold ourselves back. Only by returning to obedience can we stop damming our progress. Obedience really, truly is a great privilege and blessing.

Let us conclude this chapter with a bit of advice that applies to those who work with youth. I retrieved it from a talk delivered by Grady Bogue, who has been recognized several times in *Vital Speeches of the Year.* He is a university professor who connects well with his students, and every talk of his I have read reflects the wisdom and practicality of a great teacher.

Grady quoted from Elspeth Huxley's 1959 novel, *The Flame Trees of Thika,* which includes these beautiful lines: "The best way to find things out is not to ask questions at all. If you fire off a question it is like firing off a gun—bang it goes, and everything takes flight and runs for shelter; but if you are quite still and pretend not to be looking, all the little facts will come and peck around your feet, situations will venture forth from thickets, and intentions will creep out and sun themselves on a stone; and if you are very patient, you will see and understand a great deal more than the man with the gun does" (January 1, 1997).

This is especially true when working with youth. We can find out a lot by being with them, being aware, and being patient. We will learn much. Of course, there is a time to ask questions, but we must learn to judge the ebb and flow of conversation.

Hopefully, each of us who works with youth will understand that "the great prince of darkness / a tenfold exertion will make, / when he sees you go to the fountain, / where freely the truth you may take" (*Hymns* [Salt Lake City: The Church of Jesus Christ of Latter-day Saints, 1948], no. 21). We are in a battle—shield to shield, sword to sword—with Lucifer and his armies. The prize is the youth of the Church.

May we be able to say, when our calling working with youth is finished, as Paul did toward the end of his ministry: "I have fought a good fight, I have finished my course, I have kept the faith: Henceforth, there is laid up for me a crown of righteousness, which the Lord, the righteous judge, shall give me at that day: and not to me only, but unto all them also that love his appearing" (2 Timothy 4:7–8).

22

Elect Ladies

You blessed women who serve the young women of the Church, would you help them to seek to become elect ladies? I hope this chapter will give some insight into the life of each young woman you serve, so you may help her understand that *elect lady* is one of the most honored of all titles of women.

It came to me during the writing of this book that we will need an entire generation of sisters in this Church who qualify as elect in the eyes of God in order to pull our young men and young women through the most difficult time in history. God bless you elect ladies who lead Zion's youth as you help qualify another generation of young women who may also one day be called the elect of God. There are great hosts of elect sisters who serve in every capacity in the Church. Others serve in their homes in a quiet, blessed way.

During a recent mission presidents' seminar, we wanted to honor the wives of the mission presidents. I composed a poem and entitled it "An Elect Lady":

> The hand of God dost rest on thee
> And all that thou dost do,
> For thou has proven faithful now,
> Elect and pure and true.
> Thy children thou hast left behind

Thy home and all thou hast,
And all thy friends and womankind
Are somewhere in the past.
Grandchildren all are far away
The joys and songs they sing,
Thou hidest feelings from the day
That night doth surely bring,
And when the tears bedim thine eyes
And thy sweet heart doth long for home,
'Tis then on wings thy longing flies
Across the myriad waves of foam . . .
To them.

I want this day to honor the hosts of elect ladies who unfortunately feel that we refer only to prominent women in the Church when we refer to the elect. The dictionary defines *elect* as "chosen, select, or choice." An elect lady is one who lives according to the Lord's standards. Many sisters in the Church have their private list of those they would consider to be the elect. Typically, those lists would not include their own name, however, as many sisters feel unworthy of or inadequate for such a lofty title.

I want to talk to all of you wonderful, sweet sisters who endlessly, unwearyingly, and consistently bless all whose lives you touch. Some sisters have had to fight with every last breath to keep going. Some sisters have lived with various kinds of abuse, a loss of self-esteem, and a sense of worthlessness. Others have suffered beyond belief from loneliness, abandonment, and overwhelming responsibility when divorce takes place. So many innocent women in this Church carry on and on and on when they have little or no hope.

I met a nurse in New York. The stake president told me that she was supporting two missionaries in the field. He told me she was divorced and that her husband had not helped the family in any financial way since then. This divorced woman faithfully gave the bishop $750 a month to support her son and daughter on missions. She had not asked for help—just swallowed hard and did what had to be done. She paid a full tithing and a fast offering. The rent in New York is very high, as are her utilities and other living costs. She would never tell, but one can imagine that her meals are lean, simple, and inexpensive. Her clothing would last until her missionaries came home, and she would not take much for herself. As the stake president told me about this good sister, a lump came to my throat with an overwhelming feeling of compassion for this elect lady of God.

Many great and noble deeds are done by women whom the world would define as insignificant and unknown. They have a profound impact on those they serve. We don't know much about them but always feel secure knowing they are there.

Jacob, whom the Lord called Israel, gives insight into the influence women have. The scriptures describe Rachel as beautiful and well favored. Jacob promised Laban, the father of Rachel, that he would serve him for seven years if he would let him marry Rachel. Then we find one of the most sublime verses in all the Old Testament: "And Jacob served seven years for Rachel; and they seemed unto him but a few days, for the love he had to her" (Genesis 29:20).

My own sweet, humble mother would never have supposed that she was an elect lady. Before the divorce and after, she went to work at Garfield Smelter. She wore overalls, a man's flannel shirt, and heavy men's logging boots with metal toes. She worked like a man and somehow set aside her femininity to do what had to be done to support five sons and two daughters. Generally she worked the graveyard shift, which required her to be up all night. I think she did this so she could be home to get us children up for school and to prepare breakfast, lunch, and dinner. We came home from school for lunch at noon. She was always up. I do not know when this poor woman slept. To seven children, if ever there was an elect lady, it was Mom. Yet, she would never have dared to suppose that she would qualify for such a title.

We often refer to the widow's mite. A great principle is taught by the example of this solitary woman who simply gave "all her living." You can mentally create a picture of this poor, bedraggled woman slipping her mite into the treasury—head bowed and shoulders rounded, with faltering footsteps and ragged clothing, humble, shy, meek, and destitute.

Imagine when the widow someday leaves this existence, humbled, meek, possibly not even daring to raise her eyes to look upon the Holy Being who awaits with love and compassion to welcome this elect lady. One look from his all-seeing eye, and the hunger, loneliness, trials, and poverty will all be swept away and replaced with eternal joy. "Oh then, my beloved . . . , come unto the Lord, the Holy One. Remember that his paths are righteous. Behold, the way for man is narrow, but it lieth in a straight course before him, and the keeper of the gate is the Holy One of Israel; and he employeth no servant there; and there is none other way save it be by the gate; for he cannot be deceived, for the Lord God is his name" (2 Nephi 9:41).

There are women in every ward who are a modern-day expression of the widow offering her all, two mites! (See Mark 12:42.) Only a few recognize who they are. The bishops know.

President Naeata serves as president of the Papua New Guinea Port Moresby Mission. When he was a young man, on the day he departed for his mission, his mother came to him and said, "I am giving you all the money we have in this world for your mission." She handed him 50 cents. He served a two-year mission, living with members, as is common in Samoa. It is doubtful that he ever received any other money from anyone else in two years. A wonderful, elect lady gave all she had to her son so he could serve a mission.

Sophocles said, "One must wait until the evening to see how splendid the day has been." So it is with many people. Years ago my Aunt Beryl Hollindrake told me of her special love for her grandmother, my great-grandmother. She said: "I learned to love the Savior sitting on my grandmother's knee. She wept as she described the agony of the Savior when the cruel spikes were driven into his hands and feet." Aunt Beryl had a beautiful voice. She often sang at church and other special events. Toward the end of her life I would drop in on her in her home in American Fork. Her first husband had been killed in an automobile accident. Then she married another wonderful man, Vern Hollindrake. In her later years, as I sat in her home, I could still feel the power of her own feelings for the Savior. I loved being near her. I loved sitting and visiting with her whenever she would invite me to come by for lunch. My great-grandmother may never know the influence she has had on me through my Aunt Beryl—two elect ladies who would also protest if they were referred to as elect.

Years ago when I was in my twenties, we lived in Edgehill Ward. The ward was divided, and one of the best men I have every known, C. Elliott Richards, and his family ended up in Wasatch 2nd Ward. I think at that time they had seven or eight children. After the division, of course, the new ward needed to be entirely staffed from scratch. Margaret Richards, Elliott's wife, was called to be the ward Relief Society president. Some may have wondered at the call, given the number of children she was caring for in her own home. This elect lady filled her calling in a royal way. She was loved by the sisters and was filled with compassion and understanding, and in her bosom was a deep and abiding testimony of the Master. Using the principles of the widow's mite as a measuring rod of her time, she gave it all.

Mildred Bradley is the dear wife of Ralph O. Bradley. He has served as a bishop, stake president, mission president, temple president, and regional representative, and he is presently a sealer in the Salt Lake Temple. They have 14 children and nearly 80 grandchildren. All 14 children were married in the temple. President Bradley was part owner in a furniture business, which demanded long hours. He has spent whatever time the Lord has asked in order to fill his callings. He has been an effective leader in all he was called to do. The family has not been without major tests. One of the married daughters died recently, leaving a husband and children behind. There have been trials in their business, and some of their children have been tested beyond belief. They have never murmured. Sister Bradley—a small-framed, elegant lady—is a marvel, truly a saintly, white-haired, elect mother, wife, servant of God, and angel. What a tower of strength!

Nobility of character comes from a lifetime of making wise decisions. Most of the elect women in this Church will never serve as general officers in the Church. Many will never have an opportunity to pursue a degree at a university or be employed by a major company in an executive role. But they will have endlessly cooked meals, made beds, baked, ironed, done yard work, planted flowers, vacuumed, washed windows, washed laundry, furnished transportation to a thousand different activities for their children, stood silently as husbands went out to serve in a Church calling, faithfully read the scriptures with the children, held family home evenings, sat with the children in church meetings, tended to cuts and bruises, dealt with bad grades, healed wounded hearts and hurt feelings, and performed a thousand more kindly, caring acts that require the deepest and best kind of courage, which is to carry on and on and on.

God bless you elect women of the Church who will never receive a plaque or trophy or hardly a thank-you. Your reward is the wonderful monuments of well-behaved, loved, and good children who will grow up to do marvelous things.

Few know how difficult it is to manage on less than enough money and then see a son called into the mission field. And, wonder of wonder, miracle of miracles, the money is there when the missionary needs it. Only you mothers know how all of that comes together.

And lest we forget, God bless all of you wonderful sisters who have enough and to spare. You have shared from your affluence in a thousand various ways. No one will ever know how much money and assistance goes quietly from your purses to support missionaries, help members go to the temple, and bless the lives of the poor and widows.

One sweet woman whom I have known since I was five years old sent me $2,000 to help missionaries or others who might need financial assistance to go to the temple. She is not a wealthy woman, but she is wonderfully generous. She served a mission in the Washington Temple. Virginia truly is an elect lady. She has been a friend and an example for life. I spoke at her husband's funeral a few years ago and have watched her fill her life with Christian service and Christlike acts of goodness.

Every weekend at stake conferences and during every mission tour I meet the elect women of God. I see them sitting with their families, preparing meals, teaching Primary, and doing a score of other things to keep this Church running smoothly.

We love the women who live alone, those who long for motherhood but never bear children. Somehow, some way, they hide the heartache and agony and move forward, endlessly and lovingly serving others who are lonely, tending to everybody else's children. They suffer in silence. Sarah, the wife of Abraham, and Rachel, the wife of Jacob, both knew the longing and emptiness. These special sisters truly are the elect of God.

God bless every righteous, good woman in this Church. Thank God you are there. Thank God for your righteousness, service, love, caring, prayers, and marvelous example. Truly the elect women in this generation have been preserved to face the most difficult trials in any dispensation and to raise up the next special generation of youth, those who will prepare for the great and glorious second coming of the Master and Redeemer of the world.

Index

Aaronic Priesthood, 10–15, 116
Abed-nego, 79–80
Abuse: sexual, 25–26, 30, 68–75; of
    spouse, 46, 73–75; of child, 65–67;
    awareness of, 88. *See also* Incest
Activity programs, 15, 139, 148
Adultery, 72–73
Adversity, 4–5, 8
Agency, 28, 75
AIDS, 99
Air Force Reserve Officers Training Corp
    (AFROTC), 81–83
Alcoholism, 60–61
Anger, 20
Arnell, Larraine, 7–8
Athletics, 55–56, 145–46
Atonement: reality of, 9; requirements of,
    17; claimed through mercy, 21–22;
    for innocent suffering, 30, 65–66,
    71–72, 135–36; understanding, 45,
    54, 116–17
Attitude, 115

Babylon, 97–99
Balance, 145, 148
Baptisms for the dead, 43
Basketball, 55
Beard, Dan, 109–10
Beauty, 137–40
Behavior, 132
Benson, Ezra Taft, 101–2

Blessings, 7–8, 13
Blindness, 57–58
Bodies, 43, 79–80, 84–85
Body piercing, 88–89
Bogue, Grady, 8, 108–9, 151
Book of Mormon, 33
Boy Scouts of America, 88. *See also*
    Scouting
Bradley, Mildred, 156
Bradley, Ralph O., 156
Broken heart, 64
Brown, Hugh B., 40

Caring, 123–25
Carr, John, 32
Carter, Gene, 126
Character, 55–59, 130–36
Chardin, René de, 128
Charity, 19, 135
Chastity, 5–6
Children, 5, 65–75
Christianity, 87
Church of Jesus Christ, 11–12, 61,
    71–72
Communication, 49–54, 143–46
Computers, 143–45
Confrontation, 97–99
Consequences, 27
Convictions, 37–41
Courage, moral, 55–56
Cowley, Matthew, 115

Creations, 109–12, 137–38
Cummings, Horace, 46

Daniel, 79–80
Dawson, George, 109
Discernment, 20
Dishes, washing, 62
Divorce, 60–65
"Don't Send My Boy," 86
Draper, Mike, 64–65
Drug use, 96–98

Earrings, 88–90
Eason, George, 123–25
Ecuador woman, 28–29
Edman, Wilford, 123
Educational institutions, 101–3
"Elect Lady, An," 152
Equality, 58
Evangelists, television, 56
Evils, 48–50
Examples: teaching by, 7–8; of good
    communication, 51; of righteous
    living, 89–90; set by teachers, 105–6;
    set by Scout leaders, 110; of kindness,
    130–36

Faith, 19–20, 23
Faust, James E., 130
Featherstone, David, 70
Featherstone, Joseph, 28–29
Featherstone, Merlene, 28, 125–26
Featherstone, Vaughn J.: daughter of, 4;
    mother of, 61–63, 154
Flake, Dennis, 126
Flake, Lawrence, 126
Fletcher, Floyd, 126
Forgiveness, 8–9, 19–26, 30, 72

Galanos, John, 37–39
Gangs, 98
Gardner, John, 110, 139
Garland, Hamlin, 109
Gender identity, 71
God, justice of, 20–23
"God Pains with Their Tears," 65–66
Golden Owls, 55

Gospel of Jesus Christ, 61
Guilt, 17

Hafen, Bruce R., 144
Hanks, Marion D., 3–4
Harassment, 50
Hatred, 20
Healing, 7–8
Health, 80, 146–47
Hinckley, Gordon B., 42, 104, 130
Hollindrake, Beryl, 155
Holy Ghost: helps discern, 20; learning
    to have, 53; prompting from, 69,
    82–83, 91, 99, 104
Home, 51–52, 68, 146, 150
Homosexuality, 50, 70–71, 91
Humility, 19
Hunter, Howard W., 44
Huxley, Elspeth, 108–9, 151

"If," 83–84
Immorality, 56–57
Incest, 17–21, 24
Infirmities, 18
Influence, 139–40
Innocents, suffering of, 17–26, 30, 32,
    65, 71–72
Integrity, 58–59
Internet, 145

Jacob (Israel), 3–4, 154
Jernigen, Kenneth, 57–58
Jesus Christ: suffering of, 17–18; fulfilled
    demands of justice, 24; testimony of,
    38–40; suffered for innocents, 65–66,
    71–72
Johnstone, Margaret Blair, 32
Joseph (of Egypt), 3–4
Joy, 27–33, 148–49
Judah, 4
Judgments of God, 21, 32
Justice, 16–26, 30

Kimball, Spencer W., 43, 102–3, 144–45
Kindness, 129–36
Kipling, Rudyard, 83–84

Language, 49–54
Lazarus, Emma, 61
Laziness, 118
Leaders, priesthood, 20–21
Lee, Harold B., 44
Lewis, C. S., 55, 148–50
Little League, 70
Longhorns, Texas, 55
Love, 5, 31–32, 123–25, 149

Maeser, Karl G., 102
Malone, Walter, 8
Manti Temple, 44
Marriage, 73–75
Marsh, Thomas, 113
Maxwell, Neal A., 100
McConkie, Britt, 75
McConkie, Bruce R., 105
McKay, David O., 31–32, 52, 99, 125
McKay, Emma Ray, 31–32
Media, 87, 132, 144
"Men without Chests," 56–57
Mercy, 8–9, 16–26
Meshach, 79–80
Missionaries, 28–29, 38–39, 43–44,
    113–19
Monson, Thomas S., 130
"Mormon's Book," 33
Murder, 25, 95–97
Mutual, 146

Naeata, Mosese, 29–30, 155
Nature, 107–11, 138
Nelson, Russell M., 47, 134–35
Nofinger, Terry, 107–8

O'Connor, Dennis, 144
Obedience, 28–33, 106, 151
Olsen, Merlyn, 126
"Opportunity," 8–9
Ordinations, 13

Packer, Boyd K., 53–54, 69, 89, 99,
    100–101, 104–5
Parents, 51–52, 64–68
Patriotism, 7
Payne, Steve, 80–81

Peace, 19, 23–24, 69–70
Pedophiles, 70, 87–89
Peer influence, 51–52
Pehrson, Paul, 131
Pericles, 6
Persecution, 50
Peterson, Mark E., 69
Peterson, Wilfred, 117–18
Philippines, stories from, 7, 45–47
Philmont Ranch, 110
Poetry, 84
Politicians, 56
Prayer, 81–83, 107–8
Pride, 66–67
Profanity, 49–50, 52

Rachel, 3–4, 154
Ramos, General, 7
"Rape of Lucrece, The," 6–7
Rebelliousness, 94–99, 105–6, 150
Rector, Hartman, Jr., 83
Reeve, Rex C., 123
Repentance, 17–19, 21, 24, 45, 53
Reproving, 90–91
Resources, spiritual, 5
Revenge, 20
Reynolds, Bruford, 108, 111
Richard, C. Elliott, 155–56
Richard, Margaret, 156
Rigdon, Sidney, 39
Road rage, 97–98
Roberts, B. H., 46
Role models, 110. See also Examples
Roles, gender, 46
Romney, Marion G., 70
Rose, 137–38
"Run and Not Be Weary," 81–83

Sacrament, 10–11
Santos, Bishop, 46
Satan, 19–20, 51, 69, 91–92, 149–51
Schofield, Perry, 60–61
Scouting, 14–15, 107–11, 146–47. See
    also Boy Scouts of America
Scriptures, 54, 90
Second Coming, 48–50
Seminary, 51–52, 100–6

Sermon on the Mount, 108
Service, 10–11, 54, 82–83, 115, 118–19
Shadrach, 79–80
Shakespeare, William, 6–7
Shepherds, 126–28
Sill, Sterling W., 40, 114–15
Sin: giving in to, 6–7; not repenting of,
    16–17; consequences of, 27; poem
    on, 40; against children and wives,
    65–67; sexual, 69–73
Smith, Joseph, 39, 46–47
Smith, Joseph (of Idaho), 131–32
Smith, Joseph F., 92–93
Social skills, 118
Soldier, story of, 25–26
Speech, free, 49–50
Spiritual experiences, 53–54, 137–40
Sports, 15
Statue of Liberty, 61
Suffering: of innocents, 17–19, 30, 32; of
    transgressors, 18–19, 23–24, 45
Suicide, 149
Swan, Allen, 123
Synthonics Technologies, 144

Tanner, N. Eldon, 52
Tattoos, 88
Teachers, seminary, 104–5
Technology, 144–45

Temple marriage, 74–75
Temple work, 4–5
Temples, 42–47, 130
Temporal service, 10–11
Temptation, 5–7, 91–92
Tenure, 126
Testimony, 38–41, 125
Time, 125–26
Training, 125
Transgressors, 17–21, 24–25
Trust, 69–70

Victims, 17–21, 24
Virtue, 5–6, 94–96
Vulnerability, 70

Washington Temple, 43
Wicked, 98–99
Wilcox, Ella Wheeler, 5–6
Williams, Robert, 146
Wirthlin, Joseph B., 116
Women, 87, 152–57
Word of Wisdom, 79–83
Work, 117
World War II, 7
Worthiness, 45–46, 116

Young Women's Program, 12–14